W9-BHN-475

WILLIAMS-SONOMA

snow country cooking

Good Food for the Great Outdoors

Recipes by
Diane Rossen Worthington

Photography by
Chris Shorten

TIME
LIFE
BOOKS

TIME-LIFE BOOKS
Time-Life Books is a division of Time-Life Inc.
Time-Life is a trademark of Time Warner Inc. U.S.A.

Time-Life Custom Publishing
Vice President and Publisher: Terry Newell
Vice President of Sales and Marketing: Neil Levin
Director of Acquisitions: Jennifer L. Pearce
Director of Financial Operations: J. Brian Birky

WILLIAMS-SONOMA
Founder and Vice Chairman: Chuck Williams
Associate Book Buyer: Cecilia Michaelis

WELDON OWEN INC.
Chief Executive Officer: John Owen
Chief Operating Officer: Larry Partington
Vice President International Sales: Stuart Laurence
Series Editor: Hannah Rahill
Managing Editor: Sarah Putman
Consulting Editor: Norman Kolpas
Beverage Recipes: Lisa Atwood
Copy Editor: Sharon Silva
Art Director: Diane Dempsey
Production Director: Stephanie Sherman
Production Manager: Christine DePedro
Production Editor: Kathryn Meehan
Design Concept: Patty Hill
Food and Prop Stylist: Heidi Gintner
Assistant Food Stylist: Michael Procopio

In collaboration with Williams-Sonoma
3250 Van Ness Ave., San Francisco, CA 94109

A WELDON OWEN PRODUCTION
Copyright © 1999 Weldon Owen Inc.
814 Montgomery Street, San Francisco, CA 94133
All rights reserved, including the right of
reproduction in whole or in part in any form.

Library of Congress
Cataloging-in-Publication Data

Worthington, Diane Rossen.
   Snow country cooking: good food for the great outdoors /
recipes by Diane Worthington : photography by Chris Shorten
   p. cm.—(Williams-Sonoma Outdoors)

   Includes index.
   ISBN 0-7370-2028-8
   I. Outdoor cookery. I. Title. II. Series.
TX823.W669 1999
641.5′78—dc21   98-13761
                                   CIP

First Published in 1999
10 9 8 7 6 5 4 3 2 1

Manufactured by Toppan Printing Co., (H.K.) Ltd.
Printed in China

A NOTE ON WEIGHTS AND MEASURES
All recipes include customary U.S. and metric measurements.
Metric conversions are based on a standard developed for these
books and have been rounded off. Actual weights may vary.

A NOTE ON NUTRITIONAL ANALYSIS
Each recipe is analyzed for significant nutrients per serving. Not
included in the analysis are ingredients that are optional or added
to taste, or are suggested as an alternative or substitution either in
the recipe or in the recipe introduction. In recipes that yield a range
of servings, the analysis is for the middle of that range.

introduction

"All finite things reveal infinitude:

The mountain with its singular bright shade

Like the blue shine on freshly frozen snow,

The after-light upon ice-burdened pines . . ."

—THEODORE ROETHKE

the environment

From birds gathering at a seed-filled feeder on a snow-laden branch to a field clad in powdery white, nature's splendors add to the pleasure of dining in snow country. To help preserve the environment for future visitors, tread lightly, making sure to leave no lingering trace of your presence.

Snow country is a place for savoring life's pleasures. In grand lodge and modest cabin alike, the cold, crisp surroundings sharpen your senses. Food looks and smells more seductive, luring you with the promise of warmth, comfort, and fuel for the day's activities. From breakfast breads to midday soups and sandwiches, hearty dinners to homey desserts, good food is central to the enjoyment of winter's glories.

A Note on High-Altitude Cooking

If your retreat is above 3,000 feet (1,000 meters), you'll need to alter some recipes to compensate for the effects of reduced air pressure. Only a few adjustments are necessary. When baking, reduce baking powder and soda (bicarbonate of soda) by ⅛–¼ teaspoon per 1 teaspoon, decrease sugar by ½–1 teaspoon per 1 cup (8 oz/250 g), and add 1–2 tablespoons more liquid per 1 cup (8 fl oz/250 ml). Lengthen cooking times for foods that are boiled, and increase baking temperatures by 15–25°F (8–10°C).

setting the scene

Whether the scene is a dining room, a fireside table for two, or a picnic table in the woods, snow country meals call for coziness. You can easily create that feeling with the tabletop items you choose. Serve breakfast drinks in heavy mugs that will keep coffee and hands warm. Rustic pottery is ideal for lunchtime soups and evening stews. Complement dishware with sturdy cutlery and textured linens. To decorate the table, bring in pinecones and boughs. In the evening add candles and a wood fire to light the scene.

Bringing Meals Outdoors

Whether for practicality or pleasure, some snow country meals are eaten outdoors and call for accessories that make such ventures more manageable. Thermoses keep soups or beverages hot. Sealable plastic containers safeguard sandwiches and salads and minimize trash. Bring along lightweight plastic plates and cutlery and paper napkins or towels. A blanket or throw can double as a tablecloth and lap-warmer.

While most people associate snow country with vigorous outdoor activities, great enjoyment is also found at a beautifully set dinner table or in a comfortable chair beside the fireplace, equipped with a cozy blanket, a good book, and a steaming beverage. After a day out in the elements, treat yourself to the pleasures of the hearth.

the snow country pantry

The better stocked your retreat is, the less equipment and food-stuffs you'll have to carry with you. If you own the lodge or cabin, keep staples on hand. Basics such as hot-drink fixings supply nearly instant comfort. Items with long shelf lives, such as nuts in their shells, provide nourishing snacks with little effort. If you're renting, seek out a well-equipped place from an agent or owner who can provide detailed kitchen inventories. Bring along fresh produce to enjoy between meals and to use as colorful centerpieces.

The recipes in this book have been developed with the goal of making cooking in snow country as easy and pleasurable as possible. Most of the ingredients called for are sold in well-stocked food stores everywhere. An emphasis has been placed on convenience, reducing food preparation time.

A little advance planning will pay off greatly in the ease with which your meals are prepared. Before you go, decide on the recipes you'll cook and then make separate lists of the ingredients and the equipment you'll need. Check these lists against inventories of your lodge or cabin kitchen to determine what you'll have to bring with you. When shopping, keep an eye out for high-quality ingredients that will shorten your time in the kitchen, from fresh salsas found in the refrigerated case to preshredded cheeses to scatter atop a pizza. You can even chop vegetables or marinate meat before you leave and pack them in airtight containers.

For evening meals, consider bringing along a stove-top grill pan, which gives you results reminiscent of outdoor grilling without your having to brave the weather.

beverages

irish coffee

8 teaspoons sugar, or to taste

½ cup (4 fl oz/125 ml) whiskey

2 cups (16 fl oz/500 ml) hot brewed coffee, or as needed

½ cup (4 fl oz/125 ml) heavy (double) cream, lightly beaten to form soft peaks

❄ Place 2 teaspoons sugar in each of 4 medium-sized glass mugs. Add 2 tablespoons whiskey to each mug, then fill with coffee. Holding a spoon rounded side up over each mug, slowly pour the cream over the spoon, floating it on each mug.

serves four | per serving: calories 207 (kilojoules 869), protein 1 g, carbohydrates 10 g, total fat 11 g, saturated fat 7 g, cholesterol 41 mg, sodium 14 mg, dietary fiber 0 g

hot apple cider

4 cups (32 fl oz/1 l) apple cider

3 lemon zest strips, each ¾ inch (2 cm) wide and 2 inches (5 cm) long

2 cinnamon sticks, broken in half

6 whole cloves

1 teaspoon allspice berries

4 teaspoons brown sugar

½ cup (4 fl oz/125 ml) heavy (double) cream

2 tablespoons granulated sugar

½ cup (4 fl oz/125 ml) tuaca liqueur or Puerto Rican rum

ground cinnamon

❄ In a saucepan over medium-high heat, combine the cider, lemon zest, cinnamon sticks, cloves, allspice, and brown sugar. Bring to a boil, stirring to dissolve the sugar. Reduce to medium-low and simmer for 20 minutes. Meanwhile, whisk the cream with the granulated sugar until soft peaks form. Add 2 tablespoons tuaca or rum to each of 4 warmed mugs. Pour the hot cider through a sieve into the mugs. Top with whipped cream and ground cinnamon.

serves four | per serving: calories 263 (kilojoules 1,105), protein 1 g, carbohydrates 41 g, total fat 11 g, saturated fat 7 g, cholesterol 41 mg, sodium 22 mg, dietary fiber 0 g

hot buttered rum

3 tablespoons brown sugar

1½ tablespoons unsalted butter, at room temperature

⅛ teaspoon each ground nutmeg, cinnamon, and cloves

¾ cup (6 fl oz/180 ml) rum

2 cups (16 fl oz/500 ml) boiling water

4 cinnamon sticks

❄ In a small bowl, stir together the brown sugar, butter, nutmeg, cinnamon, and cloves. Distribute evenly among 4 warmed mugs. Add 3 tablespoons rum to each cup, then fill with the boiling water, stirring well. Garnish with cinnamon sticks.

serves four | per serving: calories 175 (kilojoules 735), protein 0 g, carbohydrates 11 g, total fat 4 g, saturated fat 3 g, cholesterol 12 mg, sodium 5 mg, dietary fiber 0 g

chai

2 cinnamon sticks, broken in half

8 allspice berries

4 whole cloves

2 peppercorns

4 cups (32 fl oz/1 l) water

16 cardamom pods, lightly crushed

4 slices fresh ginger, lightly crushed

2 tea bags or 1 tablespoon black tea

½ cup (4 fl oz/125 ml) milk, or to taste

3 tablespoons honey, or to taste

❄ With a mortar and pestle, coarsely grind the cinnamon sticks, allspice, cloves, and peppercorns. In a saucepan, combine the ground spices, water, cardamom pods, and ginger. Bring to a boil, reduce heat to medium-low, cover, and simmer for 10 minutes. Set aside, covered, for 10 minutes. Add the tea bags or loose tea in a tea ball to a teapot. Return the spiced water to a boil and pour into the teapot. Let steep for 2–3 minutes, then strain the tea and serve with milk and honey on the side.

serves four | per serving: calories 73 (kilojoules 307), protein 1 g, carbohydrates 16 g, total fat 2 g, saturated fat 1 g, cholesterol 4 mg, sodium 20 mg, dietary fiber 0 g

snuggler

⅓ cup (3 oz/90 g) plus 1 tablespoon sugar

¼ cup (¾ oz/20 g) unsweetened cocoa powder

4 cups (32 fl oz/1 l) milk

½ cup (4 fl oz/125 ml) heavy (double) cream

¼ cup peppermint schnapps

2 peppermint candies, lightly crushed

❄ In a saucepan over medium heat, combine the ⅓ cup (3 oz/90 g) sugar, the cocoa powder, and milk. Heat, stirring, until steaming. Meanwhile, whisk the cream with the 1 tablespoon sugar until soft peaks form. Remove the cocoa from the heat and add the peppermint schnapps. Pour into 4 warmed mugs or goblets and top with whipped cream and crushed candies.

serves four | per serving: calories 353 (kilojoules 1,483), protein 10 g, carbohydrates 37 g, total fat 20 g, saturated fat 12 g, cholesterol 75 mg, sodium 134 mg, dietary fiber 2 g

glögg

1 bottle (24 fl oz/750 ml) dry red wine

1¼ cups (10 fl oz/310 ml) brandy

12 whole cloves

6 cardamom pods, lightly crushed

2 cinnamon sticks, broken in half

½ cup (4 oz/125 g) sugar

4 orange zest strips, each ¾ inch (2 cm) wide and 2 inches (5 cm) long

½ cup (3 oz/90 g) raisins

¼ cup (1½ oz/45 g) blanched almonds

❄ In a saucepan over medium heat, combine the wine, brandy, cloves, cardamom pods, and cinnamon sticks. Bring to a simmer and simmer for 15 minutes. Stir in the sugar and orange zest. Divide the raisins and almonds among 4 warmed cups or goblets. Pour in the spiced wine through a sieve and serve.

serves four | per serving: calories 556 (kilojoules 2,335), protein 3 g, carbohydrates 51 g, total fat 6 g, saturated fat 1 g, cholesterol 0 mg, sodium 14 mg, dietary fiber 2 g

breakfast and brunch

apple crumb cake

1 cup (8 oz/250 g) unsalted butter, at room temperature, cut into 1-inch (2.5-cm) pieces, plus ⅓ cup (3 oz/90 g), melted

¾ cup (6 oz/185 g) firmly packed dark brown sugar

1¼ cups (10 oz/310 g) granulated sugar

2 teaspoons ground cinnamon

⅛ teaspoon ground ginger

⅛ teaspoon ground nutmeg

⅛ teaspoon ground allspice

4½ cups (22½ oz/695 g) unbleached all-purpose (plain) flour

1 teaspoon salt

1 teaspoon baking powder

1 cup (8 fl oz/250 ml) milk

2 eggs

2 teaspoons vanilla extract (essence)

2 Granny Smith or Fuji apples, peeled, cored, and cut into ½-inch (12-mm) pieces

about 1 teaspoon confectioners' (icing) sugar (optional)

✳ Preheat an oven to 375°F (190°C). Grease a 9-by-13-inch (23-by-33-cm) baking pan with butter.

✳ In a large bowl, combine the 1 cup (8 oz/250 g) cut-up butter, the brown sugar, ½ cup (4 oz/125 g) of the granulated sugar, the cinnamon, ginger, nutmeg, and allspice. Using a pastry blender or 2 knives, cut in the butter until the mixture resembles coarse crumbs. Add 2½ cups (12½ oz/385 g) of the flour and, using your fingers, crumble the mixture together to make large crumblike pieces. Set aside.

✳ In another large bowl, stir together the remaining 2 cups (10 oz/310 g) flour, the remaining ¾ cup (6 oz/185 g) granulated sugar, salt, and baking powder. In a large measuring pitcher, whisk together the melted butter, milk, eggs, and vanilla. Pour the egg mixture over the flour mixture and stir just to combine. Add the apples and stir again just to combine. Spoon the batter evenly into the prepared pan, smoothing the top. Sprinkle the brown sugar mixture evenly over the batter, lightly pressing it into the batter.

✳ Bake until the topping is crisp and the cake is springy to the touch, about 45 minutes. Remove from the oven and let cool. Dust with confectioners' sugar, if desired. The cake is best eaten the day it is made.

serves ten | per serving: calories 682 (kilojoules 2,864), protein 9 g, carbohydrates 99 g, total fat 28 g, saturated fat 17 g, cholesterol 115 mg, sodium 322 mg, dietary fiber 2 g

▲ For high-altitude cooking tips, see page 10.

winter omelet with zucchini, mushrooms, and gruyère

for the filling:

2 tablespoons unsalted butter

1 shallot, minced

1 tablespoon olive oil

½ lb (250 g) fresh mushrooms,
 brushed clean and thinly sliced

2 zucchini (courgettes), trimmed
 and julienned

2 tablespoons finely chopped fresh
 parsley

salt and ground pepper to taste

for the omelets:

12–18 eggs (2 or 3 per person)

salt and ground pepper to taste

6 tablespoons (3 fl oz/90 ml) plain
 soda water

6 tablespoons (3 oz/90 g) unsalted
 butter

6 tablespoons (1½ oz/45 g) finely
 shredded Gruyère cheese

❊ To make the filling, in a frying pan over medium heat, melt the butter.
Add the shallot and sauté until softened, about 2 minutes. Increase the heat
to medium-high and add the oil. Add the mushrooms and sauté until
slightly softened, about 3 minutes. Add the zucchini and continue to sauté
until softened, about 3 minutes longer. Add the parsley, salt, and pepper.
Remove from the heat and cover to keep warm.

❊ To prepare each omelet, in a bowl, whisk together 2 or 3 eggs, salt, pepper,
and 1 tablespoon soda water until smooth. Melt 1 tablespoon of the butter
in an 8-inch (20-cm) omelet pan or frying pan, preferably nonstick, over
medium heat. When it begins to sizzle, pour in the egg mixture and stir it
in the center with a wooden spatula. With the spatula, lift the edges of the
egg mixture so the uncooked portion runs to the edge of the pan. Vigorously
slide the pan back and forth over the heat until the eggs begin to slip freely
in the pan.

❊ When the eggs are lightly cooked but still creamy in the center, spoon
one-sixth of the filling over the omelet. Sprinkle 1 tablespoon of the
Gruyère cheese over the filling. Shake the pan; if the omelet does not slip
easily, carefully loosen the edges with the spatula. Slide the omelet onto a
plate and, when halfway out, quickly flip the pan over to fold the omelet in
half. Serve immediately. Repeat with the remaining eggs and filling until
all the omelets have been made.

serves six | per serving: calories 398 (kilojoules 1,672), protein 22 g, carbohydrates 4 g,
total fat 33 g, saturated fat 16 g, cholesterol 687 mg, sodium 217 mg, dietary fiber 0 g

french toast with pecan maple syrup

Be sure to soak the bread slices thoroughly in the egg mixture to create a custardy interior and golden brown outer layer. Besides challah, other breads that work well include whole-wheat (wholemeal) bread, sourdough, and French bread.

for the syrup:

¼ cup (1 oz/30 g) coarsely chopped
   pecans
1 cup (11 oz/345 g) maple syrup

for the french toast:

1½ cups (12 fl oz/375 ml) milk
4 eggs
1 teaspoon vanilla extract (essence)
1 tablespoon sugar
8 thick slices egg bread such as
   challah, each ¾ inch (2 cm) thick
3 tablespoons unsalted butter

❊ To make the syrup, in a frying pan over medium heat, toast the pecans, stirring often, until lightly browned and fragrant, about 3 minutes. Add the syrup and warm for about 2 minutes longer. Transfer to a heatproof pitcher and reserve. (If you like your syrup hot, you can reheat it in a microwave oven for 1 minute just before serving.)

❊ To make the French toast, in a bowl, whisk together the milk, eggs, vanilla, and sugar until well blended. Arrange the bread slices in a single layer in a large rectangular baking dish with 2-inch (5-cm) sides. (You may have to do this in batches.) Pour the egg mixture over the bread and turn the slices to coat evenly. Let the bread stand for 5 minutes.

❊ In a large frying pan over medium heat, melt 1½ tablespoons of the butter. When the foam subsides, add half of the bread slices in a single layer. Cook until golden brown, 2–4 minutes. Turn the bread over and cook on the second side until golden, about 2 minutes longer. Transfer to warmed individual plates; keep warm. Repeat with the remaining bread and butter.

❊ Serve hot, drizzled with the syrup.

serves four | per serving: calories 818 (kilojoules 3,436), protein 21 g, carbohydrates 119 g, total fat 29 g, saturated fat 11 g, cholesterol 310 mg, sodium 707 mg, dietary fiber 3 g

oatmeal with granola and dried cranberries

If you're in a hurry to head for the slopes, this easy porridge is the answer. A quick-cooking oatmeal combined with your favorite store-bought granola delivers a wonderful contrast of textures. Try raisins, currants, or diced apricots in place of the cranberries. Serve with warmed milk and brown sugar.

3½ cups (28 fl oz/875 ml) milk

2 teaspoons vanilla extract (essence)

1 teaspoon ground cinnamon

½ cup (3½ oz/105 g) firmly packed brown sugar

2 cups (6 oz/185 g) quick-cooking rolled oats

½ cup (2 oz/60 g) sweetened dried cranberries

½ cup (3 oz/90 g) store-bought granola

1 teaspoon grated orange zest

❋ In a saucepan over medium heat, combine the milk, vanilla, cinnamon, and brown sugar. Whisk to blend, then bring to a simmer. Add the oats and cook, stirring constantly, for 1–2 minutes. The timing will depend upon how thick you like your oatmeal. Add the cranberries, granola, and orange zest and stir to combine.

❋ Spoon into individual bowls and serve immediately.

serves four | per serving: calories 723 (kilojoules 3,037), protein 23 g, carbohydrates 121 g, total fat 17 g, saturated fat 8 g, cholesterol 30 mg, sodium 127 mg, dietary fiber 12 g

▲ For high-altitude cooking tips, see page 10.

breakfast crêpes with strawberry jam

1 cup (5 oz/155 g) unbleached
  all-purpose (plain) flour
1 tablespoon granulated sugar
1½ cups (12 fl oz/375 ml) milk,
  plus extra if needed to thin
3 eggs

2 tablespoons unsalted butter,
  melted, plus about 2 tablespoons
  unmelted
1 teaspoon vanilla extract (essence)
½ cup (5 oz/155 g) strawberry jam
about 1 tablespoon confectioners'
  (icing) sugar

❋ In a blender, combine the flour, sugar, 1½ cups (12 fl oz/375 ml) milk, eggs, the 2 tablespoons melted butter, and vanilla. Process until well blended. Pour into a measuring pitcher with a spout, cover, and refrigerate for 2–4 hours. Check the batter before you begin cooking. If it is thick and sluggish, thin with a bit of milk or water to the consistency of heavy (double) cream.

❋ Place an 8- or 9-inch (20- or 23-cm) nonstick frying pan over medium heat and add enough of the 2 tablespoons butter to coat lightly. When hot, pour in 2–3 tablespoons of the batter and tilt the pan, swirling the batter until the pan bottom is evenly covered. Pour any excess batter back into the pitcher. Cook until bubbles appear on the surface, about 1 minute. Flip the crêpe and cook on the second side until just set, 10–20 seconds longer. Turn out onto a plate lined with waxed paper. Cook the remaining batter in the same way, adding butter to the pan as needed and placing waxed paper between the crêpes as they are stacked. You should have about 12 crêpes.

❋ Spread each crêpe evenly with 2 teaspoons of the jam. Fold the crêpe over once and then again so that the crêpe is folded into quarters.

❋ In a large nonstick frying pan over medium heat, melt 1 teaspoon of the butter. Add 4 filled crêpes and sauté, turning once, until browned on both sides, 1–1½ minutes on each side. Transfer to a warmed platter. Repeat with the remaining butter and crêpes.

❋ To serve, arrange 2 or 3 crêpes on each warmed individual plate. Dust with confectioners' sugar. Serve immediately.

serves four to six | per serving: calories 320 (kilojoules 1,344), protein 9 g, carbohydrates 48 g, total fat 11 g, saturated fat 6 g, cholesterol 150 mg, sodium 86 mg, dietary fiber 1 g

breakfast potatoes with onions and peppers

While these potatoes are delicious served with scrambled eggs, fried eggs, or even poached eggs, they are equally at home on a dinner table with roast chicken, lamb chops, or a grilled steak.

2 tablespoons unsalted butter, plus extra if needed

2 tablespoons olive oil, plus extra if needed

1 large yellow onion, finely chopped

½ small red bell pepper (capsicum), seeded and finely diced

½ small green bell pepper (capsicum), seeded and finely diced

2 lb (1 kg) red or white boiling potatoes, peeled and cut into ½-inch (12-mm) cubes

salt and ground pepper to taste

2 tablespoons finely chopped fresh parsley

❋ In a large frying pan over medium-high heat, melt 1 tablespoon of the butter with 1 tablespoon of the olive oil. Add the onion and cook, stirring occasionally, until golden brown and just beginning to caramelize, 5–7 minutes. Be careful not to let the onion burn. Add the red and green bell peppers and cook, stirring, until they begin to soften, 3–5 minutes longer. Transfer to a serving bowl and set aside.

❋ Add ½ tablespoon each of the remaining butter and olive oil to the same frying pan over medium-high heat. Add half of the cubed potatoes and cook, turning to brown all sides evenly, until tender, 5–7 minutes. If the potatoes seem too dry, add a little more butter or oil. Transfer the browned potatoes to the serving bowl with the other vegetables. Add the remaining ½ tablespoon each butter and olive oil and cook the remaining potatoes in the same way.

❋ Return all of the mixture to the pan. Raise the heat so that the mixture quickly warms through. Remove from the heat and season with salt and pepper. Add the parsley, stir to combine, and then return to the serving bowl. Serve immediately.

serves six | per serving: calories 201 (kilojoules 844), protein 3 g, carbohydrates 28 g, total fat 9 g, saturated fat 3 g, cholesterol 10 mg, sodium 13 mg, dietary fiber 3 g

vanilla pear dutch baby

This giant puffed pancake resembles a popover. Serve with crisp bacon, orange juice, and café au lait for a satisfying weekend brunch.

¾ cup (6 fl oz/180 ml) milk

2 eggs

½ cup (2½ oz/75 g) all-purpose (plain) flour

2 tablespoons granulated sugar

1 teaspoon vanilla extract (essence)

1 teaspoon finely chopped orange zest

1 Bosc or Anjou pear, peeled, cored, and finely chopped (about 1 cup/ 4 oz/125 g)

2 tablespoons unsalted butter

about 1 teaspoon confectioners' (icing) sugar

❋ Preheat an oven to 450°F (230°C). In a blender or in a bowl, combine the milk, eggs, flour, granulated sugar, vanilla, and orange zest. Blend or whisk until smooth. Add the pear pieces and stir to combine.

❋ Put the butter in a 10-inch (25-cm) pie dish or ovenproof frying pan and place in the oven to melt. Remove from the oven and, using a paper towel or pastry brush, brush the inside of the dish or pan to coat it evenly with the butter. Pour in the batter.

❋ Bake for 15 minutes. Reduce the temperature to 350°F (180°C) and bake until golden brown and well puffed, about 15 minutes more.

❋ Remove from the oven and dust the top generously with the confectioners' sugar. Serve immediately directly from the dish or pan.

serves two | per serving: calories 455 (kilojoules 1,911), protein 13 g, carbohydrates 55 g, total fat 20 g, saturated fat 11 g, cholesterol 256 mg, sodium 110 mg, dietary fiber 2 g

▲ For high-altitude cooking tips, see page 10.

bacon and potato frittata

For ease in serving this frittata, use a pizza cutter to cut it into wedges.
Accompany with a simple mixed-fruit salad.

6 slices bacon, cut into 1-inch
   (2.5-cm) pieces
2 tablespoons olive oil
1 lb (500 g) red or white boiling
   potatoes, peeled and cut into
   ½-inch (12-mm) dice
1 leek, white and light green parts
   only, finely chopped
1 bunch spinach, about ½ lb
   (250 g), tough stems removed

salt and ground pepper to taste
12 eggs
2 tablespoons finely chopped fresh
   parsley
1½ cups (6 oz/185 g) shredded sharp
   cheddar cheese
¼ cup (2 fl oz/60 ml) store-bought
   fresh tomato or tomatillo salsa
   (optional)
¼ cup (2 fl oz/60 ml) sour cream
   (optional)

❋ In a 10-inch (25-cm) ovenproof nonstick frying pan over medium-high
heat, fry the bacon until crisp, 6–8 minutes. Using a slotted spoon, transfer
to paper towels to drain. Pour off the drippings from the pan.

❋ Preheat an oven to 425°F (220°C). Add the olive oil to the same pan and
place over medium heat. Add the potatoes and leek and sauté, stirring frequently, until the leek is golden brown and the potatoes are tender inside
and crisp on the surface, about 20 minutes. Stir in the spinach, cover, and
cook until the spinach is wilted, 2–3 minutes. Season with salt and pepper.

❋ Meanwhile, in a bowl, whisk together the eggs and parsley. Stir in
1¼ cups (5 oz/155 g) of the cheese, the bacon, salt, and pepper.

❋ Using a spatula, flatten the potato mixture in the pan and pour the egg
mixture evenly over the top. Reduce the heat to medium-low and cook, stirring
occasionally, until the bottom is lightly set and cooked, about 7 minutes.
Sprinkle evenly with the remaining ¼ cup (1 oz/30 g) cheese.

❋ Transfer the pan to the oven and bake until the frittata is puffed and
brown, 10–15 minutes. Remove from the oven and let cool. Slide onto a
round serving platter, cut into wedges, and garnish with the salsa and sour
cream, if desired. Serve immediately.

serves six | per serving: calories 402 (kilojoules 1,688), protein 24 g, carbohydrates 16 g,
total fat 27 g, saturated fat 11 g, cholesterol 460 mg, sodium 432 mg, dietary fiber 2 g

▲ For high-altitude cooking tips, see page 10.

spiced pumpkin muffins

Serve these moist golden nuggets for breakfast or for a midafternoon snack with Hot Apple Cider (page 16).

2 cups (10 oz/315 g) all-purpose (plain) flour

2 teaspoons baking powder

½ teaspoon baking soda (bicarbonate of soda)

½ teaspoon ground cinnamon

½ teaspoon ground nutmeg

½ teaspoon ground ginger

½ teaspoon ground allspice

¼ teaspoon salt

¼ cup (2 oz/60 g) unsalted butter, at room temperature

½ cup (3½ oz/105 g) plus 2 tablespoons firmly packed dark brown sugar

½ cup (4 oz/125 g) granulated sugar

1 cup (8 oz/250 g) canned pumpkin purée

½ cup (4 fl oz/125 ml) orange juice

2 eggs

1 teaspoon finely chopped orange zest

½ cup (3 oz/90 g) golden raisins (sultanas)

❋ Preheat an oven to 350°F (180°C). Butter a 12-cup muffin tin.

❋ In a medium bowl, stir together the flour, baking powder, baking soda, cinnamon, nutmeg, ginger, allspice, and salt. Set aside.

❋ In a large bowl, using an electric mixer set on medium speed, beat together the butter and brown and granulated sugars until creamy. Reduce the speed to low and add the pumpkin, orange juice, eggs, and orange zest. Beat until well blended. Add the flour mixture and beat on low speed just until well blended. Do not overmix. Add the raisins and mix just to combine. Divide the mixture evenly among the prepared muffin cups.

❋ Bake until a toothpick inserted into the center of a muffin comes out clean, 20–25 minutes. Transfer to a cooling rack and let cool in the pan for at least 15 minutes, then turn out onto the rack. Serve warm.

makes twelve muffins | per muffin: calories 255 (kilojoules 1,071), protein 4 g, carbohydrates 47 g, total fat 6 g, saturated fat 3 g, cholesterol 48 mg, sodium 199 mg, dietary fiber 1 g

▲ For high-altitude cooking tips, see page 10.

red flannel hash

Cooking with beets can be messy. You might use gloves when peeling, and place the beets on waxed paper when cutting to make cleanup easy. Be sure to stir the hash and move the mixture around continually after the first 10 minutes of cooking to ensure a brown and crusty result.

2 beets

2½ lb (1.25 kg) white, red, or Yukon gold potatoes, peeled and finely diced

3 cups (about 1¼–1½ lb/625–750 g) finely diced cooked corned beef

½ cup (4 fl oz/125 ml) heavy (double) cream

4 tablespoons (⅓ oz/10 g) finely chopped fresh parsley

1 teaspoon Worcestershire sauce

½ teaspoon salt

¼ teaspoon cayenne pepper

2 tablespoons vegetable oil

2 leeks, white and light green parts only, finely chopped

❊ Preheat an oven to 425°F (220°C).

❊ Trim the beets but do not peel. Place in a small baking pan and add water to a depth of ¼ inch (6 mm). Seal with aluminum foil and roast until fork-tender, about 45 minutes. Remove from the oven and, when cool enough to handle, peel and finely dice. Set aside.

❊ Fill a large saucepan three-fourths full of salted water and bring to a boil. Add the potatoes and boil until nearly tender, 7–10 minutes. Drain well and place in a bowl. Add the corned beef, beets, cream, 2 tablespoons of the parsley, the Worcestershire sauce, salt, and cayenne pepper. Stir to mix well.

❊ In a large nonstick frying pan over medium heat, warm the vegetable oil. Add the leeks and sauté, stirring occasionally, until translucent, 4–5 minutes. Add the potato–corned beef mixture and mix well to distribute evenly. Spread the hash evenly in the pan, flattening with a wooden spatula. Cook until a slight crust forms on the bottom, about 10 minutes. Occasionally run the spatula around the edge of the pan to keep the potatoes from sticking. Turn the mixture over and continue cooking, stirring frequently to break up the hash, until crusty and browned, 12–14 minutes longer.

❊ Spoon the hash onto warmed serving plates and garnish with the remaining 2 tablespoons parsley. Serve immediately.

serves eight | per serving: calories 409 (kilojoules 1,718), protein 18 g, carbohydrates 30 g, total fat 24 g, saturated fat 3 g, cholesterol 97 mg, sodium 1,076 mg, dietary fiber 3 g

▲ For high-altitude cooking tips, see page 10.

breakfast polenta

Full bodied and rustic, this hearty hot cereal will warm you up and fortify you for your day ahead. A dollop of sour cream and brown sugar swirled into each serving brings out the sweet flavor of the polenta. Serve with crisp bacon or sausages.

3 cups (24 fl oz/750 ml) milk
½ teaspoon vanilla extract (essence)
¾ cup (4 oz/125 g) instant polenta
⅓ cup (2½ oz/75 g) firmly packed
　dark brown sugar

for the topping:
¼ cup (2 oz/60 g) firmly packed
　dark brown sugar
¼ cup (2 fl oz/60 ml) sour cream

❊ In a saucepan over medium-high heat, combine the milk and vanilla and bring to a boil. Add the polenta, reduce the heat to medium-low, and stir continuously with a wooden spoon until slightly thickened, about 3 minutes. Stir in the brown sugar, mixing well.

❊ Spoon into cereal bowls and top with the brown sugar and sour cream, dividing them evenly. Serve immediately.

serves four | per serving: calories 358 (kilojoules 1,504), protein 9 g, carbohydrates 61 g, total fat 9 g, saturated fat 6 g, cholesterol 32 mg, sodium 110 mg, dietary fiber 3 g

banana-oatmeal waffles

These homey waffles have a moist, cakelike interior. You may find
a dusting of confectioners' (icing) sugar is all you need to sweeten them,
although maple syrup is always a treat.

1 cup (5 oz/155 g) all-purpose
  (plain) flour
1 cup (3 oz/90 g) quick-cooking
  rolled oats or 1 cup (6 oz/185 g)
  multigrain cereal
2 tablespoons firmly packed
  brown sugar
1 tablespoon baking powder
½ teaspoon baking soda
  (bicarbonate of soda)
½ teaspoon ground cinnamon

pinch of ground allspice
pinch of ground nutmeg
½ teaspoon salt
1 cup (8 fl oz/250 ml) sour cream
½ cup (4 fl oz/125 ml) milk
2 eggs
4 tablespoons (2 oz/60 g) unsalted
  butter, melted
2 ripe bananas, peeled and sliced
vegetable oil for greasing

❋ Preheat a waffle iron according to the manufacturer's directions.

❋ In a large bowl, stir together the flour, oats or cereal, brown sugar,
baking powder, baking soda, cinnamon, allspice, nutmeg, and salt.

❋ In a large measuring pitcher, combine the sour cream, milk, eggs, and
melted butter and whisk with a fork until well blended. Add the sliced
bananas and mash them in well. (An old-fashioned potato masher works
well.) Don't worry if the mixture is still a little lumpy. Add the egg mixture
to the flour mixture and mix with a fork or a whisk until a smooth batter forms.

❋ Using a paper towel or pastry brush, lightly grease the waffle iron with
vegetable oil. Following the manufacturer's directions, ladle in enough
batter for 1 waffle (usually about ½ cup/4 fl oz/125 ml) spreading it around
evenly as soon as you finish pouring. Close the waffle iron and cook until
it opens easily and the waffle is golden brown on the outside and cooked
through inside. Transfer to a warmed platter and keep warm while you cook
the remaining waffles, regreasing the waffle iron as necessary. Serve hot.

makes about seven waffles | per waffle: calories 344 (kilojoules 1,445), protein 8 g, carbo-
hydrates 38 g, total fat 19 g, saturated fat 10 g, cholesterol 95 mg, sodium 512 mg, dietary fiber 2 g

stirred eggs with chives, fontina, and prosciutto

Straining the beaten eggs will ensure a light and fluffy result. Serve these elegant scrambled eggs with warm Spiced Pumpkin Muffins (page 34) and café au lait. If you're cooking for a crowd, this recipe doubles or triples well, although you will need to use a much larger pan. Cheddar, Swiss, or even goat cheese can be substituted for the fontina, while crisply cooked bacon or pancetta can stand in for the prosciutto.

8 eggs

2 tablespoons milk

salt and ground pepper to taste

1 tablespoon unsalted butter

¼ cup (1 oz/30 g) finely diced
  fontina cheese

¼ cup (1 oz/30 g) finely shredded
  prosciutto

1 tablespoon finely chopped fresh
  chives

❋ In a bowl, whisk the eggs until blended. Pour through a fine-mesh sieve placed over another bowl, making sure that the white stringy part remains in the sieve. Add the milk, salt, and pepper and stir to combine.

❋ In a saucepan over medium heat, melt the butter. Add the eggs and, using a wooden spoon, stir continuously. As the eggs begin to form curds, keep stirring until very creamy, about 3 minutes longer. Add the cheese and prosciutto and continue stirring until the eggs form thicker curds but are still creamy, 2–3 more minutes, or until desired consistency is reached.

❋ Turn the eggs into a warmed shallow bowl and garnish with the chives. Serve immediately.

serves four | per serving: calories 223 (kilojoules 937), protein 17 g, carbohydrates 2 g, total fat 16 g, saturated fat 7 g, cholesterol 448 mg, sodium 318 mg, dietary fiber 0 g

lunch

vegetable soup with aioli

for the aioli:

1 head garlic

1 tablespoon olive oil

¼ cup (2 fl oz/60 ml) mayonnaise

1 teaspoon lemon juice

salt to taste

pinch of cayenne pepper

2 tablespoons olive oil

2 leeks, white and light green parts
  only, finely chopped

3 carrots, peeled and diced

1 red or white rose potato, about
  ½ lb (250 g), peeled and diced

3 zucchini (courgettes), diced

6 fresh mushrooms, diced

½ small cabbage, shredded

7 cups (56 fl oz/1.75 l) chicken broth

⅓ cup (3 oz/90 g) canned crushed
  tomatoes

1 clove garlic, minced

¼ teaspoon dried thyme

¼ teaspoon dried oregano

salt and ground pepper to taste

½ cup (1¾ oz/50 g) dried egg noodles

3 tablespoons finely chopped fresh
  parsley

❄ To make the aioli, preheat an oven to 425°F (220°C). Cut off the top fourth of the garlic head and then score around its perimeter. Sprinkle with the 1 tablespoon olive oil. Wrap tightly in aluminum foil and place in a small baking dish. Bake until soft when pierced, 45–60 minutes. Let cool, then squeeze the soft pulp into a small bowl and mash. Add the mayonnaise, lemon juice, salt, and cayenne pepper. Mix well. Cover and refrigerate.

❄ In a large, heavy pot over medium heat, warm the 2 tablespoons olive oil. Add the leeks and sauté until they begin to soften but not color, 3–5 minutes. Add the carrots, potato, zucchini, and mushrooms and sauté until slightly softened, about 3 minutes. Add the cabbage and sauté just until softened, about 2 minutes more. Add the broth, tomatoes, garlic, thyme, oregano, salt, and pepper and bring to a boil. Reduce the heat to medium-low and simmer, uncovered, until the vegetables are tender, 20–25 minutes.

❄ Meanwhile, bring a pot three-fourths full of salted water to a boil. Add the noodles and cook until al dente (tender yet firm to the bite), about 8 minutes, or according to the package directions. Add to the soup and stir well.

❄ Ladle into warmed bowls and top each bowl with a dollop of the aioli. Garnish with the parsley and serve immediately.

serves six to eight | per serving: calories 247 (kilojoules 1,037), protein 7 g, carbohydrates 27 g, total fat 14 g, saturated fat 2 g, cholesterol 11 mg, sodium 1,123 mg, dietary fiber 4 g

▲ For high-altitude cooking tips, see page 10.

black bean chili

2 cups (14 oz/440 g) dried black
beans

3 tablespoons vegetable oil

3 yellow onions, finely chopped

5 cloves garlic, minced

¼ cup (2 oz/60 g) good-quality
chili powder

4 teaspoons dried oregano

4 teaspoons ground cumin

1 teaspoon ground coriander

1 tablespoon paprika

¼ teaspoon cayenne pepper

3 cups (24 fl oz/750 ml) vegetable
broth

1½ cups (9 oz/280 g) canned diced
tomatoes with juice

½–1 canned chipotle chile or 1 small
seeded jalapeño chile, minced

3 cups (24 fl oz/750 ml) water

1 tablespoon rice vinegar or white
wine vinegar

3 tablespoons finely chopped fresh
cilantro (fresh coriander)

salt to taste

for the garnish:

½ cup (2 oz/60 g) diced Muenster
cheese

½ cup (4 fl oz/125 ml) sour cream

6–8 fresh cilantro (fresh coriander)
sprigs

❊ Pick over the beans, discarding any stones or misshapen beans. Rinse
and drain. Place in a bowl, add plenty of water to cover, and let stand for at
least 4 hours or for up to overnight. Drain and set aside.

❊ In a heavy pot over medium heat, warm the vegetable oil. Add the onions
and sauté until softened, about 5 minutes. Add the garlic, chili powder,
oregano, cumin, coriander, paprika, and cayenne pepper and stir to combine.
Cook, stirring occasionally, about 5 minutes.

❊ Add the broth, tomatoes, chile, water, and reserved beans and bring to a
boil. Reduce the heat to low, cover partially, and cook for 45 minutes. Uncover
and continue to cook until the beans are tender, about 45 minutes longer. If
the chili is too soupy, using a potato masher, mash some of the beans to help
thicken the mixture. When the beans are ready, add the vinegar and chopped
cilantro and stir to combine. Season with salt.

❊ To serve, divide the cheese among warmed bowls and ladle in the chili.
Garnish each serving with sour cream and cilantro.

serves six to eight | per serving: calories 393 (kilojoules 1,651), protein 17 g, carbohydrates 52 g,
total fat 15 g, saturated fat 5 g, cholesterol 15 mg, sodium 661 mg, dietary fiber 12 g

▲ For high-altitude cooking tips, see page 10.

chicken and jack cheese quesadillas

3 cups (24 fl oz/750 ml) chicken
  broth or water
½ teaspoon salt, if using water
3 skinless, boneless chicken breast
  halves
4 large flour tortillas, each 10–12
  inches (25–30 cm) in diameter

2 cups (8 oz/250 g) shredded
  Monterey jack cheese
4 tablespoons (2 fl oz/60 ml)
  store-bought fresh tomato salsa,
  plus ½ cup (4 fl oz/125 ml) for serving
fresh cilantro sprigs for garnish
½ cup (4 fl oz/125 ml) sour cream

❄ In a deep frying pan or a saucepan over medium-high heat, bring the broth to a simmer. If you're using water only, add the salt. Then add the chicken breast halves and simmer until just opaque throughout, 10–12 minutes. Remove from the heat and let the chicken cool in the liquid. Lift out the chicken breasts and shred into bite-sized pieces. You should have about 2 cups (12 oz/375 g). If you used broth, reserve for another use.

❄ Spray a large nonstick frying pan with nonstick cooking spray and place over medium-high heat. When hot, place a tortilla in the pan and sprinkle with one-fourth of the shredded cheese. Top with one-fourth of the shredded chicken and 1 tablespoon of the salsa. Fold the tortilla in half, pressing down on top with a spatula. Cook until lightly browned on the underside, about 2 minutes. Turn and cook the second side until lightly browned, about 1 minute longer. Transfer to a warmed individual plate. Repeat to make 4 quesadillas in all. Garnish with cilantro sprigs and serve with the extra salsa and the sour cream.

serves four | per serving: calories 655 (kilojoules 2,751), protein 49 g, carbohydrates 42 g, total fat 32 g, saturated fat 15 g, cholesterol 145 mg, sodium 1,034 mg, dietary fiber 2 g

smoked turkey reuben sandwiches

Named after a sandwich originated at Reuben's in New York City many years ago, this American classic is updated here with smoked turkey in place of the usual corned beef. Serve Shredded Root Vegetable Salad (page 57) and some kosher dill pickles on the side.

for the dressing:

½ cup (4 fl oz/125 ml) mayonnaise

¼ cup (2 fl oz/60 ml) bottled chili sauce

1½ tablespoons sweet green pickle relish

8 slices rye bread

¼ cup (2 oz/60 g) unsalted butter, at room temperature

½ lb (250 g) Swiss cheese, grated

¼ lb (125 g) sliced smoked turkey

1 cup (6 oz/185 g) well-drained uncooked sauerkraut

❉ To make the dressing, in a small bowl, stir together the mayonnaise, chili sauce, and pickle relish until well mixed. Set aside.

❉ Lay the bread slices on a large work surface and spread one side of each slice evenly with the butter. Turn the slices over. Spread the other side of each slice evenly with the dressing.

❉ Sprinkle a bit of cheese on 4 of the dressing-spread bread slices, then lay the turkey slices over the cheese, dividing them evenly. Make sure the turkey does not hang over the edge, trimming if necessary. Spread the sauerkraut evenly atop the turkey, and then distribute the remaining grated cheese evenly over the sauerkraut. Top with the remaining slices of bread, buttered sides out, and press down firmly to compact the sandwiches.

❉ Place a large nonstick frying pan or a griddle over medium-high heat. Using a wooden spatula, carefully lift the sandwiches from the work surface and place in the hot pan or on the griddle. Grill, occasionally pressing down gently on top of each sandwich with the spatula, until the underside is golden, 4–5 minutes. Carefully turn the sandwiches over and cook, again pressing down on them, until the second side is golden and the cheese has melted, 3–4 minutes longer. Turn over one more time and cook for 2–3 minutes longer.

❉ Transfer to individual plates and serve immediately.

serves four | per serving: calories 742 (kilojoules 3,116), protein 28 g, carbohydrates 42 g, total fat 52 g, saturated fat 21 g, cholesterol 114 mg, sodium 1,438 mg, dietary fiber 5 g

four seasons pizza

for the dough:

5 teaspoons (2 packages) active dry
  yeast

1 teaspoon sugar

1 cup (8 fl oz/250 ml) lukewarm
  water (115°F/46°C)

3 cups (15 oz/470 g) all-purpose
  (plain) flour

2 tablespoons yellow cornmeal

1½ teaspoons salt

2 tablespoons olive oil

1½ cups (15 oz/470 g) favorite
  store-bought tomato-basil sauce

1 cup (4 oz/125 g) shredded
  mozzarella cheese

¼ cup (1 oz/30 g) grated Parmesan
  cheese

6 canned artichoke hearts, well
  drained and quartered lengthwise

12 Kalamata olives, pitted and halved

6 fresh small white mushrooms,
  brushed clean, stems removed, and
  thinly sliced

2 thin slices prosciutto, shredded

❄ To make the dough, in a bowl, sprinkle the yeast and sugar over ¼ cup
(2 fl oz/60 ml) of the lukewarm water and let stand until foamy, 5–10
minutes. Stir to dissolve the yeast. In a bowl, stir together the flour, cornmeal, and salt. Add the remaining ¾ cup (6 fl oz/185 ml) water and the oil to
the yeast mixture. Gradually pour the yeast mixture into the flour mixture,
stirring until the dough comes together. If it is too dry, add 1 more tablespoon water. Turn out onto a lightly floured work surface and knead briefly
until smooth. Place in an oiled bowl, turning to coat. Cover the bowl and let
the dough rise in a warm place until doubled in volume, about 1 hour.

❄ Oil a large rimless baking sheet. Punch down the dough and turn it out
onto a floured work surface. Knead briefly until smooth, then divide in half.
Press out each half into a 9-inch (23-cm) round, forming a slight rim.
Transfer to the prepared baking sheet, cover, and let rise until tripled in
height, about 30 minutes. Meanwhile, preheat the oven to 475°F (245°C).

❄ Using a fork, pierce the rounds at even intervals. Spread the tomato sauce
evenly over each. Sprinkle with the cheeses. Arrange the artichokes, olives,
mushrooms, and prosciutto in 4 quadrants over the cheeses. Place in the
oven, reduce the temperature to 425°F (220°C), and bake until the crust is
golden brown and the cheeses are melted, 25–30 minutes. Let rest for 2
minutes, then cut into wedges and serve.

makes two pizzas; serves four | per serving: calories 791 (kilojoules 3,322), protein 27 g, carbo-
hydrates 112 g, total fat 25 g, saturated fat 7 g, cholesterol 33 mg, sodium 1,931 mg, dietary fiber 6 g

▲ For high-altitude cooking tips, see page 10.

grapefruit, fennel, and mushroom salad

Winter's bounty is celebrated in this flavorful salad. Serve before Hearty Lentil Soup (facing page) with a basket of warm sourdough bread.

for the dressing:

1 shallot, finely chopped

juice of ½ pink grapefruit

1 tablespoon balsamic vinegar

½ cup (4 fl oz/125 ml) olive oil

salt and ground pepper to taste

1 large pink grapefruit

1 fennel bulb

2 heads butter (Boston) lettuce, leaves separated and torn into bite-sized pieces

4 fresh white mushrooms, brushed clean and thinly sliced

❋ To make the dressing, in a small bowl, whisk together the shallot, grapefruit juice, and vinegar. Slowly add the oil, whisking constantly until fully incorporated. Season with salt and pepper. Set aside.

❋ Using a small knife, cut a slice off the top and bottom of the grapefruit to expose the fruit. Place upright on a cutting board and slice off the peel in thick strips, cutting around the contour of the grapefruit to expose the flesh. Holding it over a bowl, cut along either side of each section, letting the section drop into the bowl. Remove any seeds and discard. Cut the sections in 1-inch (2.5-cm) pieces. Cut off the stems and feathery tops and any bruised outer stalks from the fennel bulb. Thinly slice lengthwise.

❋ Arrange the butter lettuce in a shallow salad bowl. Place the grapefruit pieces, fennel, and mushrooms on top in an attractive pattern. At the table, drizzle with the dressing, toss, and serve.

serves four to six | per serving: calories 241 (kilojoules 1,012), protein 2 g, carbohydrates 11 g, total fat 22 g, saturated fat 3 g, cholesterol 0 mg, sodium 66 mg, dietary fiber 2 g

hearty lentil soup

2 tablespoons olive oil

1 large yellow onion, finely chopped

3 carrots, peeled and finely chopped

2 celery stalks, finely chopped

3 cloves garlic, minced

2 cups (14 oz/440 g) brown lentils,
  picked over and rinsed

1½ cups (9 oz/280 g) coarsely
  chopped honey-roasted turkey

8–9 cups (64–72 fl oz/2–2.25 l)
  chicken broth

2 cups (12 oz/375 g) canned diced
  tomatoes with juice

4 tablespoons (⅓ oz/10 g) finely
  chopped fresh parsley

½ teaspoon dried thyme

1 tablespoon balsamic vinegar

salt and ground pepper to taste

for the garnish:

¼ cup (⅓ oz/10 g) finely chopped
  fresh parsley

sour cream (optional)

croutons (optional)

❋ In a 6-qt (6-l) soup pot over medium heat, warm the olive oil. Add the onion and sauté until slightly softened, about 3 minutes. Add the carrots and celery and continue to sauté until slightly softened, about 5 minutes. Add the garlic and sauté for about 1 minute longer. Add the lentils, ½ cup (3 oz/90 g) of the chopped turkey, 8 cups (64 fl oz/2 l) of the broth, the tomatoes, 2 tablespoons of the parsley, and the thyme and bring to a simmer. Reduce the heat to medium-low and cook, uncovered, stirring occasionally, until the lentils are tender, about 30 minutes. (Test for tenderness by pushing them with the back of a wooden spoon; if they break up easily, they are cooked.) Remove from the heat and let cool slightly.

❋ Working in batches, purée the soup in a blender, making sure to retain some texture. If the soup seems too thick, add another cup (8 fl oz/250 ml) broth or water to thin to desired consistency. Return to the pan over medium heat. Add the remaining 1 cup (6 oz/190 g) turkey, remaining 2 tablespoons parsley, the vinegar, salt, and pepper. Simmer for 5 minutes to blend the flavors. Taste and adjust the seasonings.

❋ Ladle into warmed bowls. Garnish with the ¼ cup (⅓ oz/10 g) parsley and with sour cream and croutons, if using. Serve at once.

serves eight | per serving: calories 297 (kilojoules 1,247), protein 23 g, carbohydrates 39 g, total fat 6 g, saturated fat 1 g, cholesterol 14 mg, sodium 1,545 mg, dietary fiber 8 g

▲ For high-altitude cooking tips, see page 10.

three-onion soup with gruyère croutons

The key here is to caramelize the onions and leeks slowly, which gives this soup an especially rich flavor. This typical bistro dish makes a substantial luncheon main course with an accompanying plate of Shredded Root Vegetable Salad (page 57).

3 tablespoons olive oil

2 large red (Spanish) onions, thinly sliced

2 yellow onions, thinly sliced

4 leeks, white part only, thinly sliced

¼ teaspoon sugar

7 cups (56 fl oz/1.75 l) chicken or beef broth

½ cup (4 fl oz/125 ml) dry white wine

2 cloves garlic, minced

1 bay leaf

¼ teaspoon dried thyme

salt and ground pepper to taste

12 baguette slices, each ¼ inch (6 mm) thick

¾ cup (3 oz/90 g) shredded Gruyère cheese

2 tablespoons finely chopped fresh parsley

❋ In a large nonaluminum pot over medium heat, warm the olive oil. Add the red and yellow onions and sauté until wilted, about 15 minutes. Add the leeks and sugar and continue cooking, stirring frequently, until caramelized, 30–45 minutes.

❋ Add the broth, wine, garlic, and bay leaf. Cover partially and simmer until the soup thickens slightly, about 30 minutes. Discard the bay leaf. Add the thyme, salt, and pepper.

❋ Meanwhile, preheat a broiler (griller). Arrange the bread slices on a baking sheet and broil (grill) until golden, 1½–2 minutes. Watch carefully to prevent burning.

❋ Ladle the soup into individual flameproof soup bowls placed on a baking sheet. Place 2 or 3 bread slices on top of each serving and sprinkle evenly with the cheese. Broil until melted and golden. Remove from the broiler, sprinkle a little parsley over the tops, and serve immediately.

serves four to six | per serving: calories 389 (kilojoules 1,634), protein 14 g, carbohydrates 45 g, total fat 18 g, saturated fat 5 g, cholesterol 19 mg, sodium 1,672 mg, dietary fiber 5 g

▲ For high-altitude cooking tips, see page 10.

tomato-rice soup

Select a good-quality canned diced tomato for the best results.
You can vary the flavor with herbs and spices such as
tarragon, basil, or curry powder.

2 tablespoons olive oil

1 yellow onion, very thinly sliced

1 carrot, peeled and very finely
 chopped

1 celery stalk, very finely chopped

¼ cup (1¾ oz/50 g) raw long-grain
 rice

1 clove garlic, minced

2 tablespoons all-purpose (plain)
 flour

3 cups (24 fl oz/750 ml) chicken
 broth

1 can (28 oz/875 g) diced tomatoes
 with juice

¼ cup (2 oz/60 g) tomato paste

½–1 teaspoon sugar

1½ cups (12 fl oz/375 ml) milk

salt and white pepper to taste

grated Parmesan cheese (optional)

❋ In a large, heavy saucepan over medium heat, warm the oil. Add the
onion and sauté until translucent, 3–4 minutes. Add the carrot and celery
and sauté until the vegetables begin to soften, 4–5 minutes longer. Add the
rice and garlic and cook, stirring, until coated with the oil, about 1 minute.

❋ Sprinkle the flour over the vegetables, reduce the heat to low, and continue to cook, stirring constantly, until the flour is incorporated, 1–2 minutes.
Add the broth, tomatoes, tomato paste, and ½–1 teaspoon sugar, depending on
the tartness of the tomatoes. Raise the heat to medium-high and bring to a
simmer. Cover partially, reduce the heat to medium, and cook, stirring occasionally, until the vegetables and rice are cooked through and the flavors are
blended, about 20 minutes. Remove from the heat and let cool slightly.

❋ Working in batches, purée the soup in a blender, making sure to retain
some texture. Return to the pan over medium heat. Add the milk, salt, and
pepper and stir to combine. Heat to warm the soup through. Taste and
adjust the seasonings.

❋ Ladle into warmed soup bowls and sprinkle with the Parmesan cheese,
if desired. Serve at once.

serves four to six | per serving: calories 223 (kilojoules 937), protein 7 g, carbohydrates 29 g,
total fat 10 g, saturated fat 3 g, cholesterol 10 mg, sodium 998 mg, dietary fiber 3 g

▲ For high-altitude cooking tips, see page 10.

shredded root vegetable salad

This light and refreshing salad can be served as is or dressed up with crumbled goat cheese. Serve with Chicken and Jack Cheese Quesadillas (page 47) or Flank Steak Sandwiches (page 60).

for the dressing:

1 shallot, finely chopped

3 tablespoons red wine vinegar

½ cup (4 fl oz/125 ml) plus
 1 tablespoon olive oil

2 teaspoons Dijon mustard

2 tablespoons chopped fresh parsley

salt and ground pepper to taste

8 carrots, peeled and shredded

4 small or 3 large beets, peeled and
 shredded

8–10 romaine (cos) lettuce leaves

16–20 cherry tomatoes

2 tablespoons finely chopped fresh
 parsley

❄ To make the dressing, in a small bowl, whisk together the shallot, vinegar, olive oil, mustard, parsley, salt, and pepper.

❄ In a bowl, combine the carrots with ¼ cup (2 fl oz/60 ml) of the dressing and let marinate for 15 minutes. In another bowl, combine the beets with the remaining dressing and let marinate for 15 minutes.

❄ Arrange the lettuce leaves on a large serving platter or individual plates. Arrange the carrots and the beets in 2 separate mounds on the lettuce. Garnish with the cherry tomatoes, arranging them around the edges. Sprinkle with the parsley and serve.

serves six | per serving: calories 253 (kilojoules 1,063), protein 2 g, carbohydrates 16 g, total fat 21 g, saturated fat 3 g, cholesterol 0 mg, sodium 109 mg, dietary fiber 4 g

german potato salad

Select a creamy-style potato like the red rose or white rose or even a Yukon gold for this hearty salad. Idaho or russet potatoes lack the correct texture. Serve the salad alongside your favorite sandwich or on its own with a glass of full-bodied Zinfandel.

2 lb (1 kg) creamy-style potatoes (see note), unpeeled

6 slices bacon, cut into 1-inch (2.5-cm) pieces

6 tablespoons (3 fl oz/90 ml) olive oil

1 yellow onion, thinly sliced

1 tablespoon sugar

2 teaspoons all-purpose (plain) flour

salt and ground pepper to taste

½ cup (4 fl oz/125 ml) water

¼ cup (2 fl oz/60 ml) cider vinegar

¼ cup (⅓ oz/10 g) minced fresh parsley, plus 2 tablespoons chopped

❋ Bring a large saucepan three-fourths full of water to a boil over high heat. Add the potatoes, reduce the heat to medium-high, and cook, uncovered, until tender but still slightly resistant when pierced with a fork, 25–30 minutes. Drain and let cool slightly, then peel and cut into slices ½–1 inch (12 mm–2.5 cm) thick. Place in a serving bowl.

❋ In a frying pan over medium-high heat, fry the bacon until crisp and brown, 6–8 minutes. Using a slotted spoon, transfer to paper towels to drain, then add to the potatoes. Pour off the drippings from the pan. Return the pan to medium heat and warm the olive oil. Add the onion slices and sauté until soft and lightly browned, 5–7 minutes. Add the sugar, flour, salt, pepper, and water and continue cooking until the dressing begins to thicken, 3–5 minutes. Add the vinegar and the ¼ cup (⅓ oz/10 g) minced parsley and cook for 1 minute longer. Taste and adjust the seasonings. Pour the dressing over the potatoes and toss gently to combine.

❋ Garnish with the chopped parsley and serve immediately.

serves four to six | per serving: calories 359 (kilojoules 1,508), protein 6 g, carbohydrates 40 g, total fat 20 g, saturated fat 4 g, cholesterol 6 mg, sodium 130 mg, dietary fiber 3 g

▲ For high-altitude cooking tips, see page 10.

flank steak sandwiches

These versatile sandwiches can be made with warm or chilled steak.
Some other good bread choices include sourdough, ciabatta,
focaccia, or rustic country bread.

for the marinade:

2 tablespoons olive oil

1 tablespoon lemon juice

1 tablespoon Dijon mustard

1 teaspoon balsamic vinegar

1 teaspoon soy sauce

salt and ground pepper to taste

1 flank steak, 2 lb (1 kg)

½ cup (4 fl oz/125 ml) mayonnaise

3 tablespoons lemon juice

2 tablespoons bottled horseradish

1 clove garlic, minced

salt and ground pepper to taste

6 onion or poppy seed rolls, split
    horizontally

12 small lettuce leaves

❄ To make the marinade, in a small bowl, whisk together the olive oil,
2 tablespoons lemon juice, mustard, vinegar, soy sauce, salt, and pepper.
Place the flank steak in a large shallow dish and smear the marinade on
both sides. Cover and refrigerate for at least 1 hour or for up to 4 hours.

❄ Meanwhile, in a bowl, stir together the mayonnaise, 3 tablespoons lemon
juice, horseradish, garlic, salt, and pepper. Cover and refrigerate until serving.

❄ Preheat a broiler (griller) or place a large ridged stove-top grill pan over
medium-high heat.

❄ Remove the steak from the marinade, place on a broiler pan, and broil
(grill), 3 inches (7.5 cm) from the heat source, turning once, 5–7 minutes
on each side for medium-rare, or until an instant-read thermometer stuck
into the thickest part registers 135°–140°F (57°–60°C). If using a stove-top
grill pan, grill, turning once, using the same timing. Transfer the steak to a
cutting board and let rest for about 10 minutes. Thinly slice against the grain.

❄ Spread the cut sides of each roll half with some of the horseradish mayonnaise. Layer the sliced steak on the bottom halves, dividing it evenly
among the rolls, and top each with 2 lettuce leaves. Drizzle a little bit more
horseradish mayonnaise over the lettuce and then close the sandwiches.
Cut in half, if desired, and serve.

serves six | per serving: calories 569 (kilojoules 2,390), protein 35 g, carbohydrates 30 g,
total fat 34 g, saturated fat 8 g, cholesterol 89 mg, sodium 480 mg, dietary fiber 0 g

turkey-ricotta burgers

Serve these moist, flavorful burgers with the classic condiments:
ketchup, mustard, mayonnaise, and chili sauce.

2 tablespoons olive oil

2 shallots, minced

2 cloves garlic, minced

1½ lb (750 g) ground (minced) turkey

⅓ cup (2½ oz/75 g) ricotta cheese

1 tablespoon Dijon mustard

2 teaspoons Worcestershire sauce

salt and pepper to taste

6 Kaiser rolls, split horizontally and
lightly toasted

6 slices fresh tomato, preferably
beefsteak

6 lettuce leaves

❄ In a frying pan over medium heat, warm the olive oil. Add the shallots
and sauté until softened, about 2 minutes. Add the garlic and cook until
softened, about 1 minute longer. Transfer to a bowl and add the turkey,
ricotta cheese, mustard, Worcestershire sauce, salt, and pepper. Mix lightly
and shape into 6 patties, each about 1 inch (2.5 cm) thick. Cover and refrigerate for at least 1 hour or for up to 4 hours.

❄ Place a ridged stove-top grill pan or a sauté pan over medium-high heat.
When hot, spray with nonstick cooking spray and add the patties. Cook on
the first side until browned and crispy, 3–4 minutes. Flip and cook on the
second side until browned and crispy, 4–6 minutes longer. Reduce the heat
to medium, cover partially, and continue to cook until opaque throughout
or until an instant-read thermometer stuck into the thickest part of a burger
registers 160°F (71°C), 2–3 minutes longer.

❄ Transfer the burgers to the roll bottoms and garnish each with a slice of
tomato and a lettuce leaf. Top with the roll tops and serve.

serves six | per serving: calories 407 (kilojoules 1,709), protein 28 g, carbohydrates 34 g,
total fat 17 g, saturated fat 4 g, cholesterol 89 mg, sodium 510 mg, dietary fiber 2 g

dinner

citrus-rosemary chicken

The secret of this delicious chicken is that it is first steamed and then roasted until the skin is brown and crisp.

1 roasting chicken, 5 lb (2.5 kg),
* wing tips removed*
salt and ground pepper to taste
1 lemon and 1 orange
1 tablespoon whole fresh rosemary
* leaves, plus 1 teaspoon finely*
* chopped*

2 tablespoons olive oil
6 cloves garlic
1½ lb (750 g) small potatoes, cut
* into 1-inch (2.5-cm) pieces*
1 leek, white and light green parts
* only, finely chopped*
1 cup (8 fl oz/250 ml) chicken broth

✳ Preheat an oven to 450°F (230°C). Season the chicken cavity with salt and pepper. Cut the lemon and the orange in half crosswise. Cut 1 lemon half in half again, and quarter half of the orange. Loosely stuff the cavity with the cut-up lemon and orange halves, the whole rosemary leaves, 1 tablespoon of the olive oil, and 3 of the garlic cloves.

✳ Squeeze the juice from the remaining orange and lemon halves into a small bowl. Mince the remaining 3 garlic cloves. Add the garlic, the remaining 1 tablespoon oil, the chopped rosemary, salt, and pepper to the citrus juice. Stir to combine. Smear the citrus mixture over the chicken, both under and all over the skin. Place the chicken, breast side up, in a large roasting pan with a lid.

✳ Add the potatoes and leek to the roasting pan, spreading them evenly on the bottom. Season with salt and pepper and then pour the broth over them. Cover, place in the oven, and cook for 1½ hours. Uncover, stir the potatoes, and continue to cook until the chicken is golden brown and the juices run clear when the thigh is pierced at the thickest part, or until an instant-read thermometer inserted into the thickest part of the thigh away from the bone registers 165°–170°F (74°–77°C), about 15 minutes longer. Transfer the chicken to a carving platter and let rest for 10 minutes. Transfer the potatoes to a platter and keep warm. Skim the fat off the pan juices and discard; pour the juices into a small pitcher.

✳ Carve the chicken, place on the platter with the potatoes, and serve. Pass the pan juices at the table.

serves six | per serving: calories 668 (kilojoules 2,806), protein 50 g, carbohydrates 25 g, total fat 40 g, saturated fat 11 g, cholesterol 156 mg, sodium 320 mg, dietary fiber 2 g

▲ For high-altitude cooking tips, see page 10.

risotto with red swiss chard and spinach

Feel free to alter this basic recipe to include the freshest produce available, such as wild and domestic mushrooms, English peas, and zucchini (courgettes). Serve the risotto as a main course or as a side dish to Ossobuco (page 87).

3 tablespoons olive oil

1 large leek, white part only, finely chopped

1 small bunch red Swiss chard, about ½ lb (250 g), leaves finely shredded and stalks thinly sliced

1 small bunch spinach, about ½ lb (250 g), tough stems removed and leaves finely shredded

salt and ground pepper to taste

5 cups (40 fl oz/1.25 l) chicken broth

½ cup (4 fl oz/125 ml) dry white wine

1½ cups (10½ oz/330 g) Arborio rice

2 tablespoons finely chopped fresh parsley

¾ cup (3 oz/90 g) grated Parmesan cheese

❅ In a deep, heavy pot over medium heat, warm 1 tablespoon of the olive oil. Add the leek and sauté until softened, about 5 minutes. Add the chard and spinach, stir well, cover, and cook, stirring once or twice, until wilted, about 3 minutes. Uncover, raise the heat, and cook off the excess liquid, about 1 minute longer. Season with salt and pepper and remove from the heat.

❅ In a saucepan over medium-high heat, combine the broth and wine and bring to a simmer. Adjust the heat so the liquid barely simmers.

❅ In a heavy 4-qt (4-l) saucepan over medium heat, warm the remaining 2 tablespoons oil. Add the rice and stir well to coat with the oil. Pour in ½ cup (4 fl oz/125 ml) of the hot liquid and, using a wooden spoon, stir until all of the liquid is absorbed, 3–5 minutes. Continue adding the liquid, ½ cup (4 fl oz/125 ml) at a time, stirring constantly and always making sure the previous liquid is absorbed before adding more.

❅ Add the reserved vegetables with the final addition of hot liquid, mix well, and cook over low heat for 2 minutes. Remove from the heat and stir in the parsley and ½ cup (2 oz/60 g) of the Parmesan cheese. Season to taste with salt and pepper.

❅ Serve immediately. Pass the remaining ¼ cup (1 oz/30 g) cheese at the table.

serves six | per serving: calories 350 (kilojoules 1,470), protein 12 g, carbohydrates 44 g, total fat 13 g, saturated fat 4 g, cholesterol 10 mg, sodium 1,170 mg, dietary fiber 5 g

hearty winter beef stew

½ cup (2½ oz/75 g) all-purpose (plain) flour

salt and ground pepper to taste

5 tablespoons (3½ oz/105 ml) olive oil

3 lb (1.5 kg) boneless beef chuck, cut into 1½-inch (4-cm) cubes

2 large yellow onions, sliced

¼ cup (2 fl oz/60 ml) red wine vinegar

2 carrots, peeled and thinly sliced

4 cloves garlic, minced

1½ cups (12 fl oz/375 ml) beef broth

1 cup (8 fl oz/250 ml) dry red wine

¼ cup (2 oz/60 g) tomato paste

¼ teaspoon dried thyme

10 sun-dried tomatoes, soaked in water to cover for 20 minutes, drained, and quartered

3 parsnips, peeled and cut into ¾-inch (2-cm) chunks

1 lb (500 g) small boiling potatoes, cut into ¾-inch (2-cm) chunks

10 oz (315 g) frozen pearl onions, thawed and drained

2 tablespoons chopped fresh parsley

❄ Combine the flour, salt, and pepper in a large bowl. In a large, deep non-stick frying pan over medium-high heat, warm 3 tablespoons of the olive oil. Dust the beef with the flour, shaking off any excess. Add the beef to the pan in batches and brown evenly on all sides, 5–7 minutes. Using a slotted spoon, transfer to paper towels to drain.

❄ Add the remaining 2 tablespoons oil to the pan over medium-high heat. Add the onions and sauté until softened, about 5 minutes. Add the vinegar and continue sautéing until caramelized, about 15 minutes. Add the carrots and sauté until nearly tender, about 3 minutes. Add the garlic and sauté for 1 minute more. Add the broth, wine, tomato paste, thyme, and sun-dried tomatoes. Raise the heat and bring to a boil. Return the beef to the pan, reduce the heat to low, cover, and simmer, stirring occasionally, until the meat is almost tender, about 1½ hours.

❄ Add the parsnips and potatoes, cover, and continue to simmer until both the vegetables and the meat are tender, about 15 minutes longer. Add the pearl onions and cook until tender, about 5 minutes longer. Adjust the seasonings. If the sauce is thin, raise the heat and reduce for a few minutes.

❄ Spoon the stew into a large serving bowl or platter. Garnish with the parsley and serve.

serves six | per serving: calories 953 (kilojoules 4,003), protein 46 g, carbohydrates 52 g, total fat 62 g, saturated fat 21 g, cholesterol 164 mg, sodium 464 mg, dietary fiber 8 g

▲ For high-altitude cooking tips, see page 10.

honey citrus salmon

These steaming packets carry a subtle sweet-and-sour Asian flavor.
Make sure to wrap the foil packages tightly so the salmon cooks evenly.
Serve with simple rice pilaf and steamed green beans.

¼ cup (2 fl oz/60 ml) lemon juice

1 tablespoon honey

1 tablespoon soy sauce

*1 tablespoon peeled and finely
  chopped fresh ginger*

1 small shallot, finely chopped

pinch of cayenne pepper

salt to taste

4 pieces salmon fillet, ½ lb (250 g) each

※ Preheat an oven to 400°F (200°C). In a small bowl, stir together the
lemon juice, honey, soy sauce, ginger, shallot, cayenne pepper, and salt.

※ Place each piece of salmon in the center of a piece of aluminum foil
large enough to enclose it fully. Evenly spoon the lemon juice mixture over
the salmon pieces. Pull up the foil, fold over the edges, and seal securely.
Place the packets on a baking sheet.

※ Bake until just opaque throughout, 15–18 minutes. The timing will
depend on the thickness of the fillets; plan on 10 minutes for each inch (2.5
cm). You can open a packet to check for doneness.

※ Using pot holders to protect your hands, place the salmon packets on
individual plates and open them to display the salmon. Serve immediately.

serves four | per serving: calories 439 (kilojoules 1,844), protein 46 g, carbohydrates 6 g, total fat
25 g, saturated fat 5 g, cholesterol 134 mg, sodium 395 mg, dietary fiber 0 g

▲ For high-altitude cooking tips, see page 10.

leg of lamb with mustard-herb glaze

Select your favorite herb combination to personalize this classic family pleaser. If fresh herbs are available, use them for the glaze and as a garnish. Potato Gratin with Caramelized Onions (page 81) and green beans make excellent accompaniments. Serve with a full-bodied Zinfandel or Merlot.

for the glaze:

½ cup (4 oz/125 g) Dijon mustard

1 tablespoon soy sauce

1 tablespoon olive oil

3 cloves garlic, minced

1½ teaspoons dried basil

¾ teaspoon dried thyme

salt and ground pepper to taste

1 leg of lamb, 5–6 lb (2.5–3 kg), trimmed of excess fat

2½ cups (20 fl oz/625 ml) water

salt and pepper to taste

✳ Preheat an oven to 350°F (180°C). To make the glaze, in a small bowl, stir together the mustard, soy sauce, olive oil, garlic, basil, thyme, salt, and pepper.

✳ Dry the lamb with paper towels and place on a rack in a roasting pan. Spoon the glaze evenly over the lamb. Pour 1½ cups (12 fl oz/375 ml) of the water into the bottom of the pan.

✳ Roast until an instant-read thermometer inserted into the thickest part of the leg away from the bone registers 135°F (57°C) for medium-rare, 1½–1¾ hours, or 140°–150°F (60°–65°C) for medium-well, about 2 hours. Check periodically to make sure there is some liquid in the bottom of the pan and add more water if necessary. Transfer the lamb to a carving board and let rest for 10 minutes.

✳ Meanwhile, place the pan on the stove top over medium-high heat and add the remaining 1 cup (8 fl oz/250 ml) water. Bring to a boil over medium heat and deglaze the pan, stirring with a wooden spoon to dislodge any browned bits on the pan bottom. Season with salt and pepper. Skim the fat from the pan juices, then pour the juices into a small pitcher or bowl.

✳ Carve the lamb into thin slices and arrange on a warmed platter. Pass the pan juices at the table.

serves six | per serving: calories 408 (kilojoules 1,714), protein 57 g, carbohydrates 1 g, total fat 17 g, saturated fat 6 g, cholesterol 178 mg, sodium 477 mg, dietary fiber 0 g

▲ For high-altitude cooking tips, see page 10.

polenta bolognese

for the sauce:

3 tablespoons olive oil

1 lb (500 g) ground (minced) sirloin

1 yellow onion, finely chopped

1 carrot, finely chopped

1 celery stalk, finely chopped

2 large cloves garlic, minced

2 oz (60 g) prosciutto, chopped

2 cans (14½ oz/455 g each) diced
   tomatoes with juice

1 can (28 oz/875 g) crushed tomatoes

3 tablespoons minced fresh parsley

½ bay leaf

1 teaspoon dried oregano

2 teaspoons dried basil

¼ teaspoon dried thyme

salt and ground pepper to taste

1 cup (8 fl oz/250 ml) dry red wine

for the polenta:

1 tablespoon olive oil

1 small yellow onion, minced

1 clove garlic, minced

7 cups (56 fl oz/1.75 l) chicken broth

½ teaspoon salt

1 cup (6 oz/185 g) corn kernels

2 cups (10 oz/315 g) instant polenta

⅓ cup (1½ oz/45 g) grated Asiago
   or Parmesan cheese, plus ½ cup
   (2 oz/60 g) for passing

½ cup (2½ oz/75 g) finely diced
   fontina cheese

❉ To make the sauce, in a large, heavy pot over medium heat, warm 1 tablespoon of the olive oil. Add the beef and sauté until browned, 4–5 minutes.
Using a slotted spoon, transfer to a bowl. Add the remaining 2 tablespoons
oil to the same pan over medium heat. Add the onion, carrot, and celery
and sauté until softened, 6–8 minutes. Add the garlic and prosciutto and
sauté until just softened, about 1 minute. Add all the remaining sauce
ingredients, cover partially, reduce the heat to medium-low, and simmer
until the sauce has a well-rounded flavor, about 45 minutes. Remove the
bay leaf. Keep warm.

❉ To make the polenta, in a deep saucepan over medium heat, warm the
olive oil. Add the onion and sauté until softened, about 5 minutes. Add the
garlic and sauté for 1 minute. Add the broth and salt and bring to a boil.
Add the corn, then slowly add the polenta in a stream while stirring.
Reduce the heat to medium-low and cook, stirring constantly, until smooth
and stiff, 3–5 minutes. Stir in the grated and diced cheeses.

❉ To serve, divide the polenta among shallow bowls and spoon the sauce
on top. Pass the extra grated cheese at the table.

serves six to eight | per serving: calories 588 (kilojoules 2,470), protein 30 g, carbohydrates 51 g,
total fat 29 g, saturated fat 11 g, cholesterol 72 mg, sodium 1,985 mg, dietary fiber 8 g

easy coq au vin

6 slices bacon, about 5 oz (155 g),
  cut into 1-inch (2.5-cm) pieces

¼ cup (1½ oz/45 g) all-purpose
  (plain) flour

salt and ground pepper to taste

3 each chicken breast halves,
  drumsticks, and thighs

5 tablespoons olive oil

¼ cup (2 fl oz/60 ml) brandy

2 cups (16 fl oz/500 ml) dry red wine

1 tablespoon tomato paste

3 cloves garlic, minced

½ lb (250 g) fresh white mushrooms,
  brushed clean and quartered

10 oz (315 g) frozen pearl onions,
  thawed and drained

1 tablespoon unsalted butter

4 carrots, peeled and cut into ¾-inch
  (2-cm) chunks

4 turnips, peeled, quartered, and cut
  into ¾-inch (2-cm) chunks

¾ cup (6 fl oz/180 ml) chicken broth

¼ cup (⅓ oz/10 g) chopped fresh
  parsley

❊ In a large, heavy pot, fry the bacon until crisp, 4–5 minutes. Using a slotted spoon, transfer to paper towels to drain. Pour off all but 1 tablespoon of the drippings from the pan. In a bowl, stir together the flour, salt, and pepper. Lightly dredge the chicken. Add 2 tablespoons of the oil to the same pan and place over medium-high heat. Brown the chicken in batches, 5–7 minutes. Pour off the drippings from the pan. Return all the chicken to the pan, add the brandy, ignite with a match, and let the flames die. Add the wine, tomato paste, and garlic. Cover, reduce the heat to medium-low, and cook until very tender and the sauce is slightly thickened, about 50 minutes. Meanwhile, in a frying pan over medium heat, warm 1 tablespoon of the oil. Add the mushrooms and sauté until softened, 3–5 minutes. Raise the heat to high, add the onions, and stir until lightly glazed, 2–3 minutes longer. Season with salt and pepper and set aside.

❊ About 20 minutes before the chicken is ready, in a large frying pan over medium heat, melt the butter with the remaining 2 tablespoons oil. Add the carrots and turnips and sauté until beginning to brown, 3–5 minutes. Add the broth, season with salt and pepper, reduce the heat to low, cover, and simmer until just tender, about 15 minutes. Uncover and boil down the liquid until it forms a glaze. Add the bacon and 2 tablespoons of the parsley. When the chicken is ready, stir in the onion-mushroom mixture and the remaining 2 tablespoons of parsley. Season with salt and pepper. Serve on a platter with the turnips and carrots arranged around the chicken.

serves four to six | per serving: calories 705 (kilojoules 2,961), protein 52 g, carbohydrates 28 g, total fat 43 g, saturated fat 11 g, cholesterol 153 mg, sodium 547 mg, dietary fiber 5 g

turkey-vegetable cobbler

A cobbler dough replaces the traditional flaky pastry for this pot pie cousin. Frozen onions cut out extra steps without sacrificing quality. Serve with a simple salad of romaine (cos) and cucumbers tossed with a mustard vinaigrette.

10 oz (315 g) frozen pearl onions, thawed and drained

3 carrots or 10 oz (315 g) baby carrots, peeled and cubed

1 cup (5 oz/155 g) fresh or thawed frozen petite English peas

8 tablespoons (4 oz/125 g) unsalted butter

1 leek, white and light green parts only, finely chopped

1 lb (500 g) fresh mushrooms, brushed clean and coarsely diced

1 cup (6 oz/185 g) frozen corn kernels, thawed and drained

4 cups (1½ lb/750 g) diced cooked turkey breast (½-inch/12-mm dice)

7 tablespoons (2½ oz/75 g) all-purpose (plain) flour

2 cups (16 fl oz/500 ml) chicken broth

1 cup (8 fl oz/250 ml) half-and-half (half cream)

salt and ground white pepper to taste

2 tablespoons finely chopped fresh parsley

2 tablespoons finely chopped fresh dill

for the cobbler dough:

1¾ cups (9 oz/280 g) all-purpose (plain) flour

1 tablespoon baking powder

¼ teaspoon salt

4 tablespoons (1 oz/30 g) grated Parmesan cheese

6 tablespoons (3 oz/90 g) chilled unsalted butter, cut into small pieces

½ cup (4 fl oz/125 ml) heavy (double) cream

1 egg, beaten

❊ Put the thawed onions in a large bowl. Bring a saucepan three-fourths full of water to a boil, add the carrots, and simmer until just tender, about 7 minutes. Using a slotted spoon, scoop out the carrots and add to the onions. If using fresh peas, return the water to a boil, add the peas, and cook until just tender, about 3 minutes. Drain well. Add the cooked fresh or thawed frozen peas to the bowl.

❊ In a frying pan over medium heat, melt 2 tablespoons of the butter. Add the leek and sauté until softened, about 3 minutes. Add the mushrooms and sauté until softened, about 3 minutes longer. Add the contents of the pan to the bowl holding the vegetables. Then add the corn and turkey to the bowl and set aside.

❄ In a large saucepan over medium heat, melt the remaining 6 table-spoons (3 oz/90 g) butter. Sprinkle in the flour and cook, stirring constantly, for about 3 minutes, making sure the flour does not darken. Slowly add the broth and half-and-half, whisking constantly, until thickened and smooth, about 4 minutes. Season with salt and pepper. Pour the sauce over the turkey-vegetable mixture, add the parsley and dill, and mix well. Taste and adjust the seasonings.

❄ Preheat an oven to 400°F (200°C). Grease a deep 9-by-13-inch (23-by-33-cm) baking dish with butter. Pour the mixture into the prepared dish.

❄ To make the dough, in a bowl, stir together the flour, baking powder, salt, and 3 tablespoons of the Parmesan. Using a pastry blender or 2 knives, cut in the butter until the mixture resembles coarse meal. Add the cream a little at a time, stirring and tossing with a fork just until the dough holds together.

❄ On a lightly floured work surface, roll out the dough into a rectangle large enough to cover the top of the baking dish. Drape it around the rolling pin and carefully lay it over the dish, folding the edges under. Alternatively, drop the dough by spoonfuls on top of the turkey-vegetable mixture, distrib-uting them evenly. Brush the dough with the beaten egg and sprinkle the remaining Parmesan evenly over the top. Place the dish on a baking sheet.

❄ Bake until the crust is browned, 30–35 minutes. Check regularly near the end of the cooking time to prevent burning. Serve immediately, directly from the dish.

serves six to eight | per serving: calories 746 (kilojoules 3,133), protein 43 g, carbohydrates 60 g, total fat 38 g, saturated fat 22 g, cholesterol 213 mg, sodium 756 mg, dietary fiber 5 g

▲ For high-altitude cooking tips, see page 10.

pork stuffed with apples and apricots

Boneless center-cut pork loin is an excellent cut for this stove-top preparation because it retains moisture during slow cooking. Ask the butcher to make a pocket in and tie each loin for ease in stuffing. Serve with roasted potatoes and braised chard.

1 pippin or other firm, tart apple, peeled, cored, and coarsely chopped

1 cup (6 oz/180 g) whole dried apricots

½ cup (4 fl oz/125 ml) dry white wine

¾ cup (6 fl oz/185 ml) apple brandy

2 boneless center-cut pork loins, about 2 lb (1 kg) each (see note)

6 tablespoons (3 oz/90 g) unsalted butter

2 tablespoons olive oil

¼ cup (2 fl oz/60 ml) heavy (double) cream

salt and ground pepper to taste

2 tablespoons finely chopped fresh parsley

❉ In a bowl, combine the apple and dried apricots. In a saucepan over medium heat, combine the wine and ½ cup (4 fl oz/125 ml) of the brandy and bring to a boil. Pour over the apple-apricot mixture and let stand until the apricots are softened, 1–2 hours.

❉ Remove about half of the fruit from the marinade and stuff it into the hole in the center of each piece of pork by pushing it through with the handle of a wooden spoon. Reserve the remaining fruit and marinade.

❉ In a pot large enough to hold both pork loins side by side, melt the butter with the olive oil over medium-high heat. Add the pork and brown evenly, 7–10 minutes. Pour in the remaining ¼ cup (2 fl oz/60 ml) brandy, ignite it with a match, and let the flames die out. Cover, reduce the heat to low, and cook until an instant-read thermometer inserted into the pork (avoid the stuffing) registers 160°F (71°C), about 45 minutes. Transfer the pork to a carving board and cover loosely with aluminum foil. Add the reserved fruit and marinade mixture to the pan juices, bring to a boil, and boil for 2 minutes. Add the cream, reduce the heat to medium, and simmer until slightly thickened, about 3 minutes. Season with salt and pepper.

❉ To serve, cut the pork into slices ½ inch (12 mm) thick and arrange on a warmed platter. Spoon on the sauce and garnish with the parsley.

serves eight | per serving: calories 688 (kilojoules 2,890), protein 47 g, carbohydrates 16 g, total fat 44 g, saturated fat 18 g, cholesterol 186 mg, sodium 143 mg, dietary fiber 2 g

potato gratin with caramelized onions

A crisp cheese topping crowns this creamy potato dish. Serve with a large green salad or with Tomato-Rice Soup (page 56) for a satisfying vegetarian supper. It is also excellent offered as an accompaniment to Leg of Lamb with Mustard-Herb Glaze (page 70).

2 tablespoons olive oil

2 large yellow onions, thinly sliced

½ teaspoon sugar

1 teaspoon balsamic vinegar

salt and ground pepper to taste

2 cups (8 oz/250 g) grated Gruyère cheese

3 tablespoons finely chopped fresh parsley

4 cloves garlic, minced

4 lb (2 kg) baking or Yukon gold potatoes, unpeeled, cut into slices ¼ inch (6 mm) thick

2 cups (16 fl oz/500 ml) chicken broth

2 tablespoons unsalted butter, at room temperature, cut into small pieces

❄ In a large frying pan over medium heat, warm the olive oil. Add the onions and sugar and sauté until browned and caramelized, about 15 minutes. Add the balsamic vinegar and cook until the liquid evaporates and the onions are very brown, about 2 minutes longer. Season with salt and pepper and set aside.

❄ Preheat an oven to 375°F (190°C). Oil a 9-by-13-inch (23-by-33-cm) baking dish. In a small bowl, combine the cheese, parsley, garlic, and pepper.

❄ Layer half of the potatoes on the bottom of the prepared baking dish. Spread the onion mixture evenly over the potatoes. Season with salt and pepper. Layer the remaining potatoes over the onion mixture and again season with salt and pepper. Pour the broth evenly over the potatoes and sprinkle the garlic-cheese mixture evenly over the top. Dot the surface with the butter. Cover with buttered aluminum foil, buttered side down.

❄ Bake for 30 minutes. Uncover and continue baking until the top is browned and crusty and the potatoes are fork-tender, about 30 minutes longer. Serve immediately, directly from the dish.

serves six to eight | per serving: calories 431 (kilojoules 1,810), protein 17 g, carbohydrates 50 g, total fat 19 g, saturated fat 9 g, cholesterol 45 mg, sodium 416 mg, dietary fiber 6 g

▲ For high-altitude cooking tips, see page 10.

braised short ribs

Serve with your favorite mashed potatoes and bottled horseradish cream. Offer a simple green salad to begin the meal.

5 lb (2.5 kg) lean beef short ribs,
  cut into 3–4-inch (7.5–10-cm)
  pieces
salt and ground pepper to taste
3 tablespoons vegetable oil
3 large yellow onions, thickly sliced
  into rings

4 carrots, peeled and sliced ½ inch
  (12 mm) thick
4 cloves garlic, finely chopped
1½ cups (12 fl oz/375 ml) beer
1 cup (6 oz/185 g) canned crushed
  tomatoes
1 teaspoon Dijon mustard

❇ Preheat an oven to 325°F (165°C). Season the ribs with salt and pepper. In a large nonstick frying pan over medium-high heat, warm 2 tablespoons of the vegetable oil. Add the ribs in batches and brown evenly on all sides, 7–10 minutes. Using tongs, transfer the ribs to paper towels to drain, then place in a large ovenproof pot.

❇ Add the remaining 1 tablespoon oil to the same frying pan and place over medium-high heat. Add the onions and cook, stirring frequently, until browned, 7–10 minutes. Add the carrots and sauté until slightly softened, 2–3 minutes. Stir in the garlic and cook until softened, about 1 minute longer. Add the beer, tomatoes, and mustard; raise the heat to high and simmer for 1 minute. Pour the tomato mixture over the short ribs, stir to combine, cover, and bake, turning the ribs every 45 minutes, until the meat is very tender, 2½–3 hours. Season with salt and pepper and serve immediately.

serves six | per serving: calories 411 (kilojoules 1,726), protein 32 g, carbohydrates 19 g, total fat 23 g, saturated fat 8 g, cholesterol 92 mg, sodium 191 mg, dietary fiber 4 g

▲ For high-altitude cooking tips, see page 10.

white bean stew

2 cups (14 oz/440 g) dried white beans such as Great Northern

2 tablespoons olive oil

1 yellow onion, finely chopped

2 cloves garlic, minced

4 cups (32 fl oz/ 1 l) chicken broth

1 cup (8 fl oz/250 ml) dry white wine

1 cup (6 oz/185 g) canned diced tomatoes, drained

¼ cup (2 fl oz/60 ml) plus 1 tablespoon balsamic vinegar

1 large bunch spinach, about 1 lb (500 g), tough stems removed and leaves torn into bite-sized pieces

salt and ground pepper to taste

¼ cup (1 oz/30 g) grated Parmesan cheese

¼ cup (1 oz/30 g) fine dried bread crumbs, toasted

1 tablespoon finely chopped fresh parsley

❄ Pick over the beans, discarding any stones or misshapen beans. Rinse and drain. Place in a bowl, add plenty of water to cover, and let soak for at least 4 hours or for up to overnight. Drain and set aside.

❄ In a heavy saucepan over medium heat, warm the olive oil. Add the onion and sauté until softened, 5–7 minutes. Add the garlic and sauté until softened, about 1 minute longer. Then add the broth, wine, tomatoes, the ¼ cup (2 fl oz/60 ml) vinegar, and the beans. Bring to a simmer, cover, reduce the heat to low, and cook until the beans are tender and beginning to fall apart, about 2¼ hours. Mash some of the beans with the back of a spoon to create a creamy consistency. Uncover, increase the heat to medium, and reduce until thickened slightly, 5–10 minutes.

❄ Add the spinach, re-cover, and cook over medium heat, stirring once, until the spinach is slightly wilted, about 3 minutes. Add the salt, pepper, and the remaining 1 tablespoon vinegar and stir to combine. Taste and adjust the seasonings.

❄ To serve, preheat a broiler (griller). Spoon the beans into a flameproof gratin dish. In a small bowl, stir together the Parmesan cheese, bread crumbs, and parsley. Sprinkle evenly over the beans. Slip under the broiler 3–4 inches (7.5–10 cm) from the heat source and broil (grill) until the top is nicely browned, 3–4 minutes. Serve immediately, directly from the dish.

serves six | per serving: calories 357 (kilojoules 1,499), protein 20 g, carbohydrates 53 g, total fat 8 g, saturated fat 2 g, cholesterol 3 mg, sodium 904 mg, dietary fiber 29 g

▲ For high-altitude cooking tips, see page 10.

sausage and chicken ragù

4 sweet or hot Italian sausages, or
  a mixture, about 1 lb (500 g)
2 tablespoons olive oil
1 lb (500 g) boneless, skinless
  chicken breasts, cut into 1-inch
  (2.5-cm) pieces
1 yellow onion, sliced
4 cloves garlic, minced
1 cup (8 fl oz/250 ml) dry red wine
1 can (28 oz/875 g) crushed tomatoes

1 can (14½ oz/455 g) diced tomatoes
  with juice
3 tablespoons chopped fresh parsley
1 teaspoon dried basil
1 teaspoon dried oregano
salt and ground pepper to taste
1½ lb (750 g) penne, fusilli, or small
  pasta shells
½ cup (2 oz/60 g) grated Parmesan
  cheese

❉ In a frying pan over medium heat, fry the sausages until evenly browned, 5–7 minutes. Using tongs, transfer to paper towels to drain. Let cool, then cut on the diagonal into slices 1 inch (2.5 cm) thick. Place in a bowl.

❉ Pour off the drippings from the pan and add 1 tablespoon of the olive oil. Add the chicken pieces in batches and sauté until evenly browned, 3–4 minutes. Transfer with a slotted spoon to the bowl holding the sausages. Add the remaining 1 tablespoon oil to the pan over medium heat. Add the onion and sauté until softened and lightly browned, about 5 minutes. Add the garlic and sauté until softened, about 1 minute.

❉ Pour in the wine and bring to a boil. Deglaze the pan, stirring with a wooden spoon to dislodge any browned bits on the pan bottom. Add the crushed and diced tomatoes, parsley, basil, oregano, salt, and pepper. Bring to a simmer, reduce the heat to medium-low, and simmer gently, uncovered, until the sauce is slightly thickened and no wine taste remains, 15–20 minutes. Add the reserved chicken and sausages and heat through, about 5 minutes. Taste and adjust the seasonings. Keep warm.

❉ Bring a large pot three-fourths full of water to a boil. Add the penne or other pasta, stir well, and cook until al dente (tender yet firm to the bite), about 10 minutes or according to package directions. Drain and place in a warmed serving bowl. Pour on the sauce, toss well, and serve. Pass the Parmesan cheese at the table.

serves six | per serving: calories 819 (kilojoules 3,440), protein 49 g, carbohydrates 99 g, total fat 24 g, saturated fat 8 g, cholesterol 93 mg, sodium 1,049 mg, dietary fiber 5 g

ossobuco

Because you can prepare this popular Italian main course completely in advance and then reheat it just before serving, it is ideal for entertaining. Serve with Risotto with Red Swiss Chard and Spinach (page 67).

6 large veal shanks, each cut crosswise into pieces 2 inches (5 cm) thick

salt and ground pepper to taste

4 tablespoons (2 fl oz/60 ml) olive oil

2 large yellow onions, finely chopped

3 carrots, peeled and finely chopped

3 large celery stalks, finely chopped

4 cloves garlic, minced

1 cup (8 fl oz/250 ml) dry white wine

2 cans (14½ oz/455 g each) diced
  tomatoes with juice

1½ cups (12 fl oz/375 ml) beef or
  chicken broth

1 orange zest strip

1 lemon zest strip, plus 2 teaspoons
  finely chopped

½ teaspoon chopped fresh thyme or
  ¼ teaspoon dried thyme

1 bay leaf

4 tablespoons (⅓ oz/10 g) finely
  chopped fresh parsley

❋ Season the veal with salt and pepper. In a large frying pan over medium-high heat, warm 2 tablespoons of the olive oil. Add the veal in batches and brown, turning once, about 4 minutes on each side. Transfer to a bowl and set aside. Preheat an oven to 325°F (165°C).

❋ In a large, deep ovenproof nonstick frying pan that will accommodate the veal in a single layer, warm the remaining 2 tablespoons oil over medium heat. Add the onions, carrots, and celery and sauté, stirring often, until all the vegetables are softened, 5–8 minutes. Add the garlic and cook until softened, about 1 minute longer.

❋ Raise the heat to high, add the wine, and cook until most of the liquid evaporates, about 2 minutes. Add the tomatoes, broth, orange and lemon zest strips, thyme, and bay leaf and then place the browned veal in a single layer in the pan. Bring to a boil, cover, and bake in the oven until all the shanks are very tender, about 1½ hours. Discard the bay leaf and citrus zest strips and stir in 2 tablespoons of the parsley. To serve, garnish with the remaining 2 tablespoons parsley and the chopped lemon zest.

serves six | per serving: calories 435 (kilojoules 1,827), protein 38 g, carbohydrates 38 g, total fat 15 g, saturated fat 3 g, cholesterol 125 mg, sodium 579 mg, dietary fiber 7 g

▲ For high-altitude cooking tips, see page 10.

desserts

roasted pears with cranberry-wine glaze

Bosc pears have a creamy texture that holds up well during cooking, making them a good choice for this rustic bistro-style dessert. Serve with Spiced Molasses Cookies (page 93) or biscotti.

1 cup (8 fl oz/250 ml) dry red wine

1 cup (8 fl oz/250 ml) cranberry
 juice cocktail

⅔ cup (5 oz/155 g) sugar

1 cinnamon stick

finely chopped zest of 1 lemon

8 ripe Bosc pears with stems
 attached

fresh mint leaves

❇ Preheat an oven to 350°F (180°C).

❇ In a saucepan over medium-high heat, combine the red wine, cranberry juice, sugar, cinnamon stick, and lemon zest. Bring to a simmer, stirring to dissolve the sugar, and cook for about 3 minutes. Remove from the heat and remove the cinnamon stick.

❇ Starting at the blossom end, core each pear (a melon baller works well for this), leaving the stem end intact. Then cut a slice off the bottoms so the pears will stand upright. Carefully wrap each pear stem in a small piece of aluminum foil to prevent burning during roasting. Stand the pears in a 9-by-13-inch (23-by-33-cm) baking dish, stem ends up. Pour the wine mixture evenly over the pears.

❇ Roast, basting every 15 minutes with the cranberry-wine sauce, until tender when pierced with a knife, about 1 hour and 20 minutes. Remove from the oven and arrange on a serving platter. Carefully remove the foil from each stem.

❇ Pour the wine mixture remaining in the baking dish into a saucepan and place over medium-high heat. Bring to a simmer and cook until reduced to a syrupy glaze, 10–15 minutes. Spoon the glaze over the pears.

❇ Garnish with the mint leaves and serve warm or at room temperature.

serves eight | per serving: calories 187 (kilojoules 785), protein 1 g, carbohydrates 48 g, total fat 1 g, saturated fat 0 g, cholesterol 0 mg, sodium 2 mg, dietary fiber 4 g

▲ For high-altitude cooking tips, see page 10.

spiced molasses cookies

Moist and chewy, these full-flavored cookies are perfumed with sweet spices. Serve with Mixed Dried Fruit Compote (page 100), fresh fruit desserts, or ice cream.

2¼ cups (11½ oz/360 g) all-purpose (plain) flour

2 teaspoons baking soda (bicarbonate of soda)

1 teaspoon ground cinnamon

1 teaspoon ground ginger

½ teaspoon ground nutmeg

½ teaspoon ground allspice

½ teaspoon ground cloves

¼ teaspoon salt

¾ cup (6 oz/180 g) unsalted butter, at room temperature

1 cup (7 oz/220 g) firmly packed dark brown sugar

1 egg

¼ cup (3 oz/90 g) molasses

about 3 tablespoons granulated sugar

❄ In a bowl, stir together the flour, baking soda, cinnamon, ginger, nutmeg, allspice, cloves, and salt.

❄ In a large bowl, using an electric mixer set on medium speed, beat together the butter and brown sugar until fluffy. Beat in the egg and molasses. Reduce the speed to low and add the flour mixture, mixing until blended. Cover the bowl and refrigerate for at least 1 hour or for up to 8 hours.

❄ Preheat an oven to 350°F (180°C). Grease 2 baking sheets.

❄ Place a large sheet of waxed paper on a work surface and sprinkle it with the granulated sugar. Using your palms, shape the dough into balls 1¼ inches (3 cm) in diameter. Then roll the balls in the granulated sugar, coating them evenly. Arrange the balls on the prepared baking sheets, spacing them about 2 inches (5 cm) apart. Using the tines of a fork, press the fork into each cookie, pushing down to create a decorative top.

❄ Bake until just set and lightly browned, 10–12 minutes. Remove from the oven and let cool on the sheets for 10 minutes. Gently transfer to racks and let cool completely. Store in an airtight container for up to 1 week.

makes about forty cookies | per cookie: calories 92 (kilojoules 386), protein 1 g, carbohydrates 14 g, total fat 4 g, saturated fat 2 g, cholesterol 15 mg, sodium 82 mg, dietary fiber 0 g

▲ For high-altitude cooking tips, see page 10.

banana chocolate bread pudding

Be sure to use a high-quality egg bread, such as a good challah or brioche. You can dry the bread cubes by putting them out on the counter overnight or in a 250°F (120°C) oven for 30 minutes.

8 cups (16 oz/500 g) day-old cubed
challah (1-inch/2.5-cm cubes)

4 oz (125 g) bittersweet chocolate,
coarsely chopped

2 bananas, peeled and sliced

6 whole eggs, plus 2 egg yolks

1¼ cups (10 oz/315 g) granulated
sugar

3 cups (24 fl oz/750 ml) milk

1 tablespoon vanilla extract
(essence)

boiling water, as needed

1 tablespoon confectioners' (icing)
sugar

whipped cream (optional)

❋ Grease a 9-by-13-inch (23-by-33-cm) glass baking dish with butter. Arrange the bread, chocolate, and bananas in the prepared dish, mixing them around and making sure they are evenly distributed.

❋ In a bowl, using an electric mixer set on medium speed, beat together the whole eggs and egg yolks until frothy. Add the granulated sugar and beat until the mixture is thick and lemon colored, about 3 minutes. Reduce the speed to low, add the milk, and beat until combined. Mix in the vanilla.

❋ Ladle the egg mixture over the bread and let stand for 30–60 minutes to allow the bread to absorb the liquid. Occasionally push down on the bread with a wooden spoon. (You can test to see if the bread cubes are absorbing the liquid by cutting into one.) Meanwhile, preheat an oven to 375°F (190°C).

❋ Place the baking dish in a large baking pan and pour boiling water into the baking pan to reach halfway up the sides of the dish. Bake until a skewer inserted into the center of the bread pudding comes out clean, 40–45 minutes. Remove from the oven, dust the top with the confectioners' sugar, and let rest for about 10 minutes.

❋ To serve, cut into squares and serve plain or with whipped cream. The bread pudding is also excellent served cold the next day.

serves six to eight | per serving: calories 613 (kilojoules 2,575), protein 17 g, carbohydrates 95 g, total fat 20 g, saturated fat 9 g, cholesterol 293 mg, sodium 435 mg, dietary fiber 2 g

▲ For high-altitude cooking tips, see page 10.

ginger applesauce cake

½ cup (4 oz/125 g) unsalted butter,
  at room temperature

1 cup (7 oz/220 g) firmly packed
  dark brown sugar

1 egg

2 cups (10 oz/315 g) all-purpose
  (plain) flour

1 teaspoon baking soda
  (bicarbonate of soda)

1 teaspoon ground cinnamon

1 teaspoon ground ginger

½ teaspoon ground nutmeg

½ teaspoon salt

3 tablespoons finely chopped
  crystallized ginger

1 cup (9 oz/280 g) unsweetened
  applesauce

¾ cup (3 oz/90 g) chopped walnuts

½ cup (3 oz/90 g) raisins

1 tablespoon confectioners' (icing)
  sugar

❊ Preheat an oven to 350°F (180°C). Oil an 8½-inch (21.5-cm) springform pan.
In a bowl, using an electric mixer set on medium speed, beat together the
butter and brown sugar until fluffy. Add the egg and beat well. In another
bowl, stir together the flour, baking soda, cinnamon, ground ginger, nutmeg,
salt, and crystallized ginger. Add to the butter-sugar mixture in three batches,
alternating with the applesauce. The batter will be thick. Add the nuts and
raisins and mix just until combined. Pour into the prepared pan.

❊ Bake until a knife inserted into the center comes out clean, about 55 minutes.
Place on a rack and let cool completely. To serve, remove the pan sides and
slide the cake onto a round platter. Dust the top with the confectioners' sugar.

serves eight | per serving: calories 478 (kilojoules 2,008), protein 6 g, carbohydrates 72 g,
total fat 20 g, saturated fat 8 g, cholesterol 58 mg, sodium 330 mg, dietary fiber 3 g

▲ For high-altitude cooking tips, see page 10.

mocha-glazed chocolate bundt cake

3 cups (15 oz/470 g) all-purpose
  (plain) flour

2 cups (1 lb/500 g) sugar

2 teaspoons baking soda
  (bicarbonate of soda)

½ teaspoon salt

½ cup (1½ oz/45 g) unsweetened
  cocoa powder

1 cup (8 fl oz/250 ml) hot water

1 cup (8 fl oz/250 ml) cold water

1 cup (8 fl oz/250 ml) plus ½ teaspoon vegetable oil

1 teaspoon vanilla extract (essence)

½ cup (3 oz/90 g) semisweet (plain)
  chocolate chips

2 tablespoons strong brewed coffee

3 oz (90 g) semisweet (plain)
  chocolate, broken into pieces

4 tablespoons (2 oz/60 g) unsalted
  butter

2 teaspoons light corn syrup

❋ Preheat an oven to 350°F (180°C). Butter and flour a lightweight 10-inch (25-cm) Bundt pan. In a bowl, sift together the flour, sugar, baking soda, and salt.

❋ Place the cocoa in a large bowl. Slowly add the hot water while stirring constantly. When smooth, stir in the cold water. Then mix in the 1 cup (8 fl oz/250 ml) of the vegetable oil and the vanilla. Whisk in the flour mixture until incorporated. Pour into the prepared pan. Sprinkle the chocolate chips evenly over the surface, then press them into the batter.

❋ Bake until the cake begins to come away from the sides of the pan, the top is springy to the touch, and a toothpick inserted into the center comes out almost clean, about 55 minutes. Transfer to a rack to cool for 30 minutes, then invert onto the rack and lift off the pan. Let cool completely.

❋ Meanwhile, in a heatproof bowl or in the top pan of a double boiler, combine the coffee, chocolate, and butter to make a glaze. Place over (not touching) simmering water in a pan and stir until melted. Add the corn syrup and the ½ teaspoon vegetable oil and stir to combine.

❋ Place the cake on the rack on a baking sheet lined with waxed paper. Drizzle the glaze evenly over the top. Transfer the cake to a platter and serve.

serves eight to ten | per serving: calories 711 (kilojoules 2,990), protein 6 g, carbohydrates 96 g, total fat 37 g, saturated fat 11 g, cholesterol 16 mg, sodium 422 mg, dietary fiber 4 g

▲ For high-altitude cooking tips, see page 10.

tarte tatin

A nonstick frying pan makes this traditional caramelized apple tart easy to turn out. Accompany each slice with a scoop of vanilla ice cream.

for the pastry:

1 cup (5 oz/155 g) all-purpose (plain) flour

1 tablespoon sugar

pinch of salt

½ cup (4 oz/125 g) chilled unsalted butter, cut into 1-inch (2.5-cm) pieces

¼ cup (2 fl oz/60 ml) ice water

for the filling:

6 tablespoons (3 oz/90 g) unsalted butter

¾ cup (6 oz/185 g) sugar

5 or 6 pippin or Granny Smith apples, peeled, quartered, and cored

❋ To make the pastry, in a bowl, stir together the flour, sugar, and salt. Using a pastry blender or 2 knives, cut in the butter until the mixture resembles coarse meal. Sprinkle with the ice water and stir and toss with a fork until the dough is evenly moistened. Turn the dough out onto a lightly floured work surface, gather it together, and shape into a disk. Roll out into an 11-inch (28-cm) round. Drape over the rolling pin and transfer to a piece of waxed paper. Cover with a second piece of waxed paper and refrigerate.

❋ Preheat an oven to 400°F (200°C). In an ovenproof 10-inch (25-cm) non-stick frying pan over medium heat, melt the butter. Stir in the sugar until almost dissolved, about 2 minutes. It may look a little lumpy. Add the apple quarters, rounded sides down, using just enough to fit snugly. Reduce the heat to low and cook until the caramel is dark brown and the apples are barely tender, about 15 minutes.

❋ Place the pan in the oven for about 5 minutes to cook the apples. Remove from the oven and raise the heat to 450°F (230°C). Carefully place the pastry round over the top, tucking the excess pastry inside the rim of the pan. Return to the oven and bake until the pastry is browned, about 20 minutes.

❋ Remove from the oven. Run a knife around the inside edge of the pan to make sure the tart will unmold easily. Invert a serving platter over the pan, then flip the pan and the platter together. Lift off the pan. Serve warm or at room temperature.

serves six to eight | per serving: calories 439 (kilojoules 4,394), protein 3 g, carbohydrates 57 g, total fat 23 g, saturated fat 14 g, cholesterol 62 mg, sodium 24 mg, dietary fiber 2 g

▲ For high-altitude cooking tips, see page 10.

mixed dried fruit compote

Cooking dried fruits in sweet wine such as Riesling brings out their sweet and slightly tart character. A small bowl of this compote, topped with whipped cream, is a satisfying ending to lunch or dinner, or is even wonderful served warm in the morning. The compote will keep for up to 5 days in the refrigerator.

for the fruit compote:
¾ lb (375 g) dried whole apricots
¾ lb (375 g) dried pitted whole prunes
½ lb (250 g) dried pitted cherries
1 Granny Smith or pippin apple, peeled, cored, and finely chopped
1 Bosc or Comice pear, peeled, cored, and finely chopped

½ cup (4 oz/125 g) sugar
2 cups (16 fl oz/500 ml) Riesling or Gewürztraminer
1½ cups (12 fl oz/375 ml) water

for the whipped cream:
1 cup (8 fl oz/250 ml) chilled heavy (double) cream
2 tablespoons confectioners' (icing) sugar

❋ In a large, heavy saucepan, combine the apricots, prunes, cherries, apple, pear, sugar, wine, and water. Bring to a boil over medium-high heat. Reduce the heat to low and simmer uncovered, stirring occasionally, until the fruits are soft and the liquid has thickened, about 25 minutes.

❋ Meanwhile, to make the whipped cream, in a bowl, whip together the cream and confectioners' sugar until soft peaks form. Transfer to a small serving dish, cover, and refrigerate until serving.

❋ When the fruits are cooked, transfer to a serving bowl and let cool until warm, or let cool completely, cover, and chill, if desired.

❋ To serve, spoon the fruit compote into individual glass bowls. Top each with a dollop of the whipped cream.

serves eight | per serving: calories 504 (kilojoules 2,117), protein 5 g, carbohydrates 97 g, total fat 15 g, saturated fat 10 g, cholesterol 31 mg, sodium 26 mg, dietary fiber 7 g

▲ For high-altitude cooking tips, see page 10.

orange sponge pudding cake

⅔ cup (5 oz/155 g) sugar

2 tablespoons unsalted butter, at room temperature

2 teaspoons finely chopped orange zest

3 eggs, separated

3 tablespoons all-purpose (plain) flour

¼ cup (2 fl oz/60 ml) strained fresh orange juice

1 cup (8 fl oz/250 ml) half-and-half (half cream)

⅛ teaspoon salt

⅛ teaspoon cream of tartar

boiling water, as needed

❈ Preheat an oven to 350°F (180°C). In a bowl, using an electric mixer set on medium speed, beat together the sugar, butter, and orange zest until creamy and well blended. Beat in the egg yolks. Stir in the flour, orange juice, and half-and-half until well blended.

❈ Fit the mixer with clean beaters. In a bowl, combine the egg whites, salt, and cream of tartar and beat on medium-high speed until stiff peaks form.

❈ Fold the egg whites into the egg yolk mixture just until incorporated. Pour into a 1-qt (1-l) soufflé dish. Set the dish in a large baking pan and pour boiling water into the baking pan to reach halfway up the sides of the dish. Bake until the pudding cake is set and the top is nicely browned, about 45 minutes. Remove from the oven. Serve immediately, spooning the pudding and cake onto individual plates.

serves four | per serving: calories 351 (kilojoules 1,474), protein 7 g, carbohydrates 45 g, total fat 17 g, saturated fat 9 g, cholesterol 197 mg, sodium 147 mg, dietary fiber 0 g

▲ For high-altitude cooking tips, see page 10.

maple-pecan tart

for the pastry:

1½ cups (7½ oz/235 g) all-purpose
(plain) flour

1 tablespoon confectioners' (icing)
sugar

9 tablespoons (4½ oz/140 g) unsalted
butter, cut into small pieces

¼ cup (2 fl oz/60 ml) water

for the filling:

½ cup (3½ oz/105 g) firmly
packed dark brown sugar

2 tablespoons all-purpose (plain)
flour

pinch of salt

½ cup (5½ oz/170 g) maple syrup

½ cup (5 oz/155 g) dark corn syrup

3 eggs

1 tablespoon unsalted butter, melted

3 cups (12 oz/375 g) pecan halves,
lightly toasted

1 tablespoon confectioners' (icing)
sugar

1 cup (8 fl oz/250 ml) chilled heavy
(double) cream

¼ cup (3 oz/90 g) maple syrup,
chilled

❄ To make the pastry, in a bowl, stir together the flour and confectioners' sugar. Using a pastry blender or 2 knives, cut in the butter until the mixture resembles coarse meal. Sprinkle with the water and toss with a fork until evenly moistened. Turn out onto a lightly floured surface, knead briefly, and shape into a disk. Enclose in plastic wrap and refrigerate for 30 minutes.

❄ Preheat an oven to 400°F (200°C). To make the filling, in a bowl, whisk together the brown sugar, flour, salt, maple syrup, dark corn syrup, eggs, and melted butter.

❄ On a floured work surface, roll out the dough into a 13-inch (33-cm) round. Transfer to an 11-inch (20-cm) tart pan, easing it into the bottom and sides. Trim the overhang even with the pan rim. Place the pan on a baking sheet. Spread the pecans in the shell. Pour in the filling and bake for about 15 minutes. Reduce the oven temperature to 350°F (180°C) and bake until the pastry is golden brown and the filling is set, 15–20 minutes longer. Transfer to a rack to cool, place on a serving platter, and remove the pan sides. Dust with the confectioners' sugar.

❄ In a bowl, whip together the cream and maple syrup until soft peaks form. Place in a serving bowl and pass at the table.

serves six to eight | per serving: calories 954 (kilojoules 4,007), protein 11 g, carbohydrates 91 g, total fat 64 g, saturated fat 21 g, cholesterol 182 mg, sodium 103 mg, dietary fiber 4 g

▲ For high-altitude cooking tips, see page 10.

chocolate brownie sundaes

¾ cup (6 oz/185 g) unsalted butter

4 oz (125 g) unsweetened chocolate, broken into pieces

4 eggs

2 cups (1 lb/500 g) sugar

1 teaspoon vanilla extract (essence)

1 cup (5 oz/155 g) all-purpose (plain) flour

½ teaspoon baking powder

½ teaspoon salt

1 cup (4 oz/125 g) chopped walnuts

for the hot fudge sauce:

8 oz (250 g) bittersweet or semisweet (plain) chocolate

½ cup (4 oz/125 g) unsalted butter

¼ cup (2 fl oz/60 ml) heavy (double) cream

1 teaspoon vanilla extract (essence)

1 teaspoon corn syrup

1 qt (1 l) good-quality vanilla ice cream

❋ Preheat an oven to 350°F (180°C). Butter a 9-by-13-inch (23-by-33-cm) baking pan. In a heatproof bowl or the top pan of a double boiler, combine the butter and chocolate. Place over (not touching) simmering water in a pan and melt together, stirring until smooth. Remove from over the water and let cool.

❋ In a bowl, using an electric mixer set on medium speed, beat the eggs until blended. Add the sugar and beat until the mixture is thick and pale yellow and will hold a trail when the beaters are lifted, about 5 minutes. Add the vanilla and the butter-chocolate mixture and stir just until no streaks remain; do not overmix. Fold in the flour, baking powder, and salt just until incorporated. Stir in the nuts. Pour the batter into the prepared pan. Bake until a toothpick inserted into the center comes out with slightly fudgy crumbs adhering to it, 25–30 minutes. Transfer to a rack and let cool. Cut into 3-by-3¼-inch (7.5-by-8-cm) brownies. You should have 12 in all.

❋ To make the hot fudge sauce, in a heatproof bowl or the top pan of a double boiler, combine the chocolate and butter. Place over (not touching) simmering water in a pan and melt together, stirring until smooth. Add the cream and whisk to incorporate. Add the vanilla and corn syrup and whisk to combine. Keep warm over hot water.

❋ To assemble, place a brownie on each plate. Place a large scoop of ice cream on each brownie and then drizzle the hot fudge sauce over the top.

serves twelve | per serving: calories 699 (kilojoules 2,936), protein 9 g, carbohydrates 73 g, total fat 46 g, saturated fat 24 g, cholesterol 150 mg, sodium 181 mg, dietary fiber 3 g

▲ For high-altitude cooking tips, see page 10.

rice pudding with dried apricots and golden raisins

Select a medium-grain rice to ensure this pudding's delicate character.

5 cups (40 fl oz/1.25 l) half-and-half (half cream)

1 cup (7 oz/220 g) medium-grain white rice

¾ cup (6 oz/185 g) granulated sugar

2 egg yolks

1 teaspoon vanilla extract (essence)

1 teaspoon finely chopped orange zest

½ cup (3 oz/90 g) dried apricots, finely chopped

½ cup (3 oz/90 g) golden raisins (sultanas)

2 tablespoons unsalted butter, at room temperature

cinnamon sugar (optional)

❄ In a large saucepan over medium-high heat, combine the half-and-half and the rice and bring to a boil. Reduce the heat to medium and simmer, stirring occasionally at the beginning and constantly the last few minutes to avoid scorching, about 18 minutes. The rice should be soft, but the mixture should be very creamy, and not all the liquid should be absorbed. Remove from the heat and add the sugar, stirring to blend completely.

❄ In a small bowl, whisk together the egg yolks, vanilla, and orange zest until blended. Stir ½ cup (3½ oz/105 g) of the hot rice mixture into the egg mixture, then return the egg yolk–rice mixture to the rice mixture, mixing well. Stir in the apricots, raisins, and butter until well combined and evenly distributed. Pour into a serving bowl and let cool to room temperature. Sprinkle with cinnamon sugar, if desired, and serve.

serves six | per serving: calories 621 (kilojoules 2,608), protein 10 g, carbohydrates 83 g, total fat 29 g, saturated fat 17 g, cholesterol 155 mg, sodium 89 mg, dietary fiber 2 g

▲ For high-altitude cooking tips, see page 10.

index

acknowledgments

The publishers and photography team wish to thank J. Goldsmith Antiques, Sue Fisher King, and Sandra Griswold, who kindly lent props for the photography, and Hellie Robertson and Sarah Hammond, who opened their homes. Thanks also to Cecily Upton, Beverly McGuire, and Ken DellaPenta for their generous assistance.

WILLIAMS-SONOMA